Presentimiento

Presentimiento

a life in dreams

Harrison Candelaria Fletcher

Autumn House Press

pittsburgh

"Autumn House Press" and "Autumn House" are registered trademarks owned by Autumn House Press, a nonprofit corporation whose mission is the publication and promotion of poetry and other fine literature.

Autumn House Press Staff

Michael Simms: Founder and President

Eva Simms: Co-Founder

Christine Stroud: Senior Editor

Alison Taverna: Managing Editor

Daniel Schwoegl: Intern

Sharon Dilworth: Fiction Editor

J.J. Bosley, CPA: Treasurer

Anne Burnham: Fundraising Consultant

Michael Wurster: Community Outreach Consultant

Jan Beatty: Media Consultant

Heather Cazad: Contest Consultant

Michael Milberger: Tech Crew Chief

Autumn House Press receives state arts funding support through a grant from the Pennsylvania Council on the Arts, a state agency funded by the Commonwealth of Pennsylvania, and the National Endowment for the Arts, a federal agency.

ISBN: 978-1-938769-13-9

Library of Congress Control Number: 2015954121

for my mother, with love

contents

acknowledgments

MANY THANKS to the editors, contest judges, and editorial staff who have supported my work.

Sections of this book, often in different forms, previously appeared in the following literary journals: "Imperfect Blossoms," *Ghost Town* (Issue 8, Fall 2015); "Transplants," *Duende* (Spring 2015); "Within The Walls," *Pacifica Review* (Winter 2015); "Portraits," *The Pinch* (Spring 2015); "House of Sun," *Sonora Review* (Spring 2014); "Artifacts," *Newfound: An Inquiry of Place* (Spring 2014); "Prayer For Rain," *Broad Street* (Spring 2014); "Sorrowful Mysteries," *Passages North* (Winter 2014); "Rescue," *upstreet* (Fall 2013); "Ascent," *TriQuarterly* (Fall 2013); "Vessels," *High Desert Journal* (Fall 2012); "Looking Glass," *South Loop Review* (Fall 2011); "A Loving Wind," *The Coachella Review* (Fall 2011); "Echo" and "Release," *Many Mountains Moving* (Spring 2010). "Prayer for Rain" also appears in the *Manifest West: A Literary Anthology* (Western Press Books, ed. Larry Meredith 2014), and "Artifacts" appears in *Best of Newfound: An Inquiry of Place* (2014).

"House of Sun" won the 2014 *Sonora Review* Essay Prize; "Vessels" won the 2012 *High Desert Journal* Obsidian Prize; "Artifacts" was nominated by *Newfound: An Inquiry of Place* for a Pushcart Prize in 2014,

"Prayer For Rain" was nominated by *Broad Street* for a Pushcart Prize 2014, and "A Loving Wind" was nominated by *The Coachella Review* for a Pushcart Prize in 2011.

I also would like to thank the following writers for their generosity, advice, support, and friendship: Dinty W. Moore, Marc J. Sheehan, Sue William Silverman, Nance Van Winckel, Re'Lynn Hansen, Brenda Miller, Barrie Jean Borich, and Mary Domenico. Thanks also to Michael Simms, Christine Stroud, and the excellent team at Autumn House Press. Most of all, I would like to thank my beautiful wife, children, and family.

"Perhaps home is not a place, but simply an irrevocable condition."

—James Baldwin

Presentimiento

Prologue

THE STONE is warm in my fingers. Round. Green. A gift from my mother, who pulled it years earlier from the white sand bluffs above the Rio Grande.

"Take it," she told me. "For your collection."

Opening my hand I heard, "Remember."

Decades from my New Mexican roots, with a wife, two children, and new life of my own, I sit at night on my front porch step in Denver, called to a land that will not let me be. I lift the stone to my face. Breathe in the dust and buffalo grass. Watch the silver dollar sun roll across a turquoise sky. My mother's face rises from the llano. Salt cedar hair. Copper eyes.

"Listen," she says. "I want to tell you something."

In August 1989, a few months before he entered the hospital for the final time, my grandfather, Carlos, visited my mother's Albuquerque house for supper. As she prepared his favorite red chile enchiladas, he leaned in the threshold of her kitchen, clutching his gray fedora. "A wonderful thing just happened to me," he said, hands trembling from Parkinson's.

A week earlier, he had been sitting at his own kitchen table when he became dizzy and blacked out. He felt arms take him. Lift him. Then he was driving. Gripping the wheel of his sky blue F-150 through a village of apricots, alfalfa, lilacs, and cottonwoods. Tires hummed beneath him. Sunlight flashed through a crack in his windshield. All at once, he felt a warmth wash over him. "I don't know how to say it," he told my mother. "Un viento amoroso. A loving wind."

"It's like this," my mother tells me. "People were very spiritual in the old days. Not like they are now. They knew spirits are all around us. When I was a girl there weren't many phones in the country. When someone died, they told you in other ways. A chair moved. A picture fell. Once my grandmother came into the kitchen and said, 'I dreamed of my friend last night lying in a coffin. Get your things. We're going to Villanueva.' Sure enough, when we got there, we found out her friend had died. It happened all the time. It's called a presentimiento. Something you feel in your heart."

When my mother speaks, her hands fold in her lap like the wings of a pale bird. She leans back in her antique rocker and the amber light of her reading lamp shines in her bifocals like two rising moons. Her voice becomes a whisper. Her words drift through the room like the piñon incense caressing her displays of relics—cowbells, skeleton keys, rusty nails, rosary beads—unlocking the stories within. When my mother speaks I enter her world completely. I see relatives I have never met, walk ground I have never visited, inhabit memories not my own. When my mother speaks, I dream.

I lead my deceased grandparents along a washboard road in the Rio Puerco badlands. Carlos shuffles through red dust in construction boots and a gray fedora. Desolina picks her way beside him, shiny black pumps, matching handbag, gripping his elbow for balance. Late summer. Early evening. The sky an orange flame. I hurry ahead, anxious to show them the resting place I have found.

"Almost there," I say over my shoulder. "Not much farther."

Desolina smiles a crooked smile and whispers in Spanish to Carlos, who nods, frowns, wipes his forehead with his khaki shirtsleeve. They pause to watch me, unsure if I know the way.

One

homing (ˈhəʊmɪŋ) ˈhōmiNG /

ORIGIN: Middle English, from Old English hām; see *tkei-* in Indo-European roots.

noun

1. (biology) The inherent ability or innate instinct of animals to return after being released

2. capable of guiding self:

- Honeybees navigate by the sun and the polarization pattern of the blue sky

- Marbled newts navigate only when stars are visible

- Mollusks feel their way along topographic contours

- Salmon retain an imprint of their natal stream and use memory to return years later

※

"It's exploring, it's judging habitats, it's making decisions, and all of the time, it's keeping an awareness of how to find a way back."

—Robin Baker

※

"It is something birds are born understanding they must do."

—Gretel H. Schueller and Sheila K. Schueller

※

"... to discount our own emotions toward home is to ignore biology itself."

—Bernd Heinrich

※

"We are drawn to where we came from."

—Eric Hoffer

Memory Box

HERE IS the valley, the small of a woman's back, an earthen hollow be-
tween the shoulder blades of Mesa Chivato and the rump of the Manzano
Mountains. The valley is the source of all life in this land and always has
been—a wellspring of crops and commerce where all roads converge be-
neath the blue dome sky. Through the valley flows a river, shallow and
brown, a bull snake in the grass. Fed by the snows of Colorado, the Rio
Grande meanders north-south through rock and stone, through patchworks of
alfalfa and green chile, before emptying into the Gulf of Mexico.

To the east, fifteen miles from the water's edge, stands Sandia Crest, a
blue granite wall rising some ten thousand feet from the valley floor. Broad
as a workman's shoulders, lined with canyons, flecked with pine, the San-
dias are a source of firewood and Christmas trees, the domain of black bear
and bald eagle. Each evening, the Sandias burn magenta in the setting sun,
bright as the watermelon flesh for which they're named. To the west, the
llano, a blanket of sand and scrub pulled tight to the chin of Mesa Prieta.
Scarred by arroyos and volcanic rock, the llano is the opposite of its sibling
kin, as barren as the river is fertile, as fickle as the mountain is steady. The
llano is the province of mirages, dust devils and black widow spiders, where
shadows spread like oil beneath the hubcap moon.

Here is the valley, shaped by Tiguex, conquistador, missionary, pilgrim.
Here is the valley. Here is home.

I arrive in a storm, in the swell of a tornado touching down seventy miles south near Socorro, city of mercy, stirring the sky over Albuquerque into an ink wash of purple and black. Wind crashes into the pines lining my mother's horseshoe driveway, showering down branches and needles. I hardly notice. My eyes are fixed instead on the house before me—a house dying, sagging in on itself like a Pueblo grandmother drawing close a shawl of cobwebs and leaves. Where honeysuckle once curled along the front porch vigas adobe stucco peels and plaster cracks grow. Painted window murals of sun gods and spirit eagles fade into dust and water stains. From behind the front curtains, I can feel my mother watching me, a shadow on glass, there and gone.

I kill the engine and step outside and up the front steps of my childhood home, past the gray statue of Saint Francis of Assisi, the pile of sun-bleached deer antlers, the brass bowl of fossilized stones, and the display wall of rusty gears, railroad spikes, cowbells, and keyholes. A black cat, a stray from the ghost town of Guadalupe, scurries from the welcome mat, squinting through golden eyes.

The screen door flaps open. My mother and I embrace. It's good to see her after nearly a decade away. She blinks up at me, owlish in her bifocals, thinner than I remember, than I want to admit, her face drawn and her auburn hair streaked white, exhausted by the long recovery from open-heart surgery. She squeezed my hand from the hospital gurney on that winter morning. Squeezed it so hard it hurt. Forcing a smile now, she returns to her place at the window.

She's worried about the wind, she tells me. The pines. The previous summer during a similar squall, the forty-foot ailanthus in her backyard toppled over and shattered her bedroom window, tossing branches as thick as telephone poles onto the Russian olive tree in the front yard, missing her car by inches. The summer before that, the sixty-foot-tall cottonwood on the south side split in half during a monsoon and crashed onto her den, cracking the rafters and ceiling plaster.

"It was horrible," she says, shuddering. "Sounded like a bomb."

The pines. I remember the pines. We transplanted them from the Pecos Wilderness when I was five or six, a few years after my father died. My mother chose five saplings in all, one for each of us kids, and spaced them evenly along the outer edge of her driveway. She wanted them for privacy, she told us, for protection against the wind, but after four decades, never trimmed, they stand three times as tall as her house, swaying with each gust like drunken giants.

"We'll be fine," I say, touching her shoulder. "The storm will pass."

"No. You don't know what it's like."

She folds her arms and turns away toward the interior of her home. I follow her eyes, half-expecting to find the room exactly as I remember—Navajo rugs, prayer poles, peacock feathers, Cochiti drums—but discover instead displays of porcelain saints, rosary beads, gilded lamps, and crucifixes. Before her surgery she told me she wanted to rid herself of trinkets and strip her home to the simplicity of a church. Although wall-to-wall artifacts remain, they're all spiritual in some way, giving the room the aura of a chapel, complete with flickering candles and a creaky wooden floor.

My mother has always been a creature of phases. Her house has always changed with the seasons. More than a refuge, it became a museum, a second-hand shop, a reliquary, and a camposanto, where artifacts came to life in my hands and I traveled back centuries. Standing here again after so long away, I realize just how little I know of this house—of her life—and how it came to be. We are all shaped by the places we live. What we inherit is not ours to decide. My mother handed me her looking glass of memory. Through its shimmering lens, I try to see us both more clearly.

Below the window I notice my favorite antique—a nickel-plated hope chest my mother bought in the '70s from a widow in the hills above Cuba, New Mexico. We had been following a cattle trail to see where it led when she stopped at a roadside adobe for directions to the highway. The old woman invited us inside and in the sitting room my mother saw the chest. Her grandmother had one like it, she said. Same camelback design. Same metalwork of butterflies and daisies. Her family must be proud. The old woman shrugged. Her daughters couldn't care less. Once the trunk held her dowry of lace and linen, but had come to store only winter blankets. If my mother liked it so much, she could have it as a gift. My mother thanked her, but offered instead to buy it with a fifty-dollar money order she planned to use for our light bill. The old woman agreed.

Back home on our porch my mother scrubbed the rusty surface with lemon oil and steel wool until it shimmered like a treasure chest. Inside it she placed her most cherished artifacts from a lifetime of collecting: beaded doe skin moccasins, Yaqui Easter masks, Tibetan prayer beads, a crown of thorns from the Penitente brotherhood, and a hand-held silver mirror, one side convex, the other concave. While she pruned her roses outside, I'd sneak over to lift the heavy trunk lid, breathing in leather and wood, and turning the mirror in my hands, playing with my dual reflection.

In the gray light of the storm, the chest seems as dull as a lead pipe, but in the lower right corner, I notice a thin coat of liquid silver painted over one of the blossom designs—my mother's attempt at restoration—but the line is crooked and the edges blurred. When

I reach out to touch it, she frowns. Her arthritis has been bothering her again, she says. Once the swelling recedes in her knuckles, she'll finish. I didn't mean to embarrass her, but before I can apologize, she moves into the den to rest, flicking off lights behind her. I watch her descend the darkened steps, then follow.

She gathers artifacts from the desert sand. Rocks, roots, barbed wire, and bones. She carries them home to build mosaics on her walls—self-portrait shrines of memory, family, landscape, and faith, each one a shard of an elusive whole. She does not know what she seeks. She does not know if she will return with full pockets. My mother ventures into the badlands with only a prayer to Saint Anthony and a belief in this—if she is meant to find something, she will. She calls it, "rescuing."

Midnight. I sit alone in the den with the creaks and cracks of the old house settling in, pines swaying outside, black cat curled in the corner. In the amber glow of a desk lamp, I read my mother's walls.

Wasp's nest. Horseshoe. Spanish sword. Crucifix. . .

Relics from a lifetime of collecting displayed like artwork on the fading white plaster.

Branding iron. Railroad spike. Bailing wire. Skeleton key. . .

Shards of who she is, who she was, who I envision her to be.

Hammer head. Weather vane. Hatpin. Holster. . .

As a boy, this was the world I inhabited—image, artifact, fragment, negative space. And this was the language she taught me to speak. While my mother sleeps away the storm, my eyes pass from one thing to another, seeking the stories within. At random, I select from a table a small brass box, one of her "memory boxes," and trace the design on the rectangular lid—an Aztec sun god ringed by twin serpents and hummingbirds. Squeaking open the hinges, I unpack the contents:

Silver cross. Made for a necklace, with small, drilled holes, so you can see the other side. All her life my mother has dreamed of dead relatives, as her mother and grandmother had. Nothing dark or ominous. Just conversations with loved ones. Like many New Mexican Catholics, she also gives away crosses as gifts of guidance and protection. "Spirits are all around," she says. "Be careful what you call to you. And allow inside." She gave me a cross like this once, but I lost it.

Scorpion pendant. Tail curled, stinger poised. When my mother was a girl on the ranch in Corrales, whatever blew in from the llano stopped at their door. Beggars. Wanderers. Outlaws. Poisonous things. My mother's grandmother, Adelida, at only four-feet-five inches tall, met them all. Once, a rattlesnake slithered into her kitchen and coiled to strike. Without a thought, the old woman set aside her apron, reached beside the stove for a coal shovel, chopped off the snake's head, and resumed work. My mother saw it all. And remembered.

Cowbell. Made of copper. Small as a thimble. Each morning on the ranch my mother woke to the calliope clunk of cattle making their own way toward the pasture along the Rio Grande. Each night, following some instinct or inner guide, the cows returned on their own, every one of them, as if they knew in their hearts where they belonged. My mother fell asleep to the muffled sounds they made to each other in the corral—squeaks and squeals and trills. She called it singing.

Dress label. *One hundred percent silk*. Pierced with needle and thread. My mother, taught by her grandmother, has always sewn—for relaxation, or as creative outlet, or a way to clothe us kids when the money ran low. On sunny afternoons she cleared the dining room table of fruit bowls and house cats and spread out bolts of cotton fabric, rice paper patterns, straight pins, and seamstress chalk. In the blue smoke of her Singer Genie, silhouettes took shape—arms and legs and torsos, like a new family of life-sized paper dolls. Culottes for my sisters. Button-down shirts for my brother and me.

"How do they fit?" she'd ask. "Let me see you."

Holding our arms wide, we'd twirl.

Sheriff's badge. Made of plastic, painted silver, and stamped with a lasso and Texas rose, bought for a buck at a trading post. After school, my siblings and I played cowboys and Indians with the neighborhood kids. We were always the Indians. Forever outnumbered, destined to lose, we charged through the sunflowers with our Russian olive spears.

Pocket bible. Black leather cover. Pages pulled loose or fallen away. When I was in the third grade my mother left the church to protest the liberal policies of the Vatican II Council. Before then we attended Mass each Sunday. I held her hand in the stained glass light, soothed by the voice of the baritone pastor, but unsure what he meant. When the pews emptied for communion, my mother handed me her purse to find chewing gum for the drive home. I unsnapped the snap and slipped my hand inside, feeling my way over the cold car keys, the pinprick fountain pen, and the buttery Mexican billfold before fishing out a stick of Doublemint. I cut it in half—one for her and one for me—then peeled off the foil wrapper to play with my blurred reflection.

A figurine. A woman of glass. On hands and knees with hair tied back and sleeves rolled at the elbows. One of my uncle's sculptures. Part of a Navajo shepherd camp he had mounted on a piece of drift-wood. One of his memory scenes shaped from Pyrex rods and a blue propane flame.

In her posture I see my mother on Saturday mornings waxing our hardwood floors. Imported from my father's family mill in Iowa, he had always stressed to her how important they were to him. Before he died, he taught her to care for them—by hand, rubbing in Johnson paste wax with a cotton cloth in tight, even circles, forcing moisture into the dry grain.

I hold the tiny woman, who shimmers like water and light, no eyes, no mouth, unreadable.

The pine trees shift outside. The black cat blinks in the corner.

I return the items to the box, but pocket the figurine.

She loved the New Mexico sun. Each morning she pulled back the window curtains to usher in the radiant light. My mother did not, however, like strangers peering into our home. Day after day she adjusted and readjusted bamboo shades, rice paper screens, and Russian olive branches nailed across the frames. Nothing worked. Especially for her room, which had twelve square panels facing north and east. At dawn, her walls blazed, but come nightfall, her room stood exposed. One morning, she uncapped her oil paints, and squeezed a curl of violet pigment onto the glass. With a palette knife and wide-bristle brush she smoothed on the paint until the front yard pines outside vanished beneath a lavender veil. Next, she chose orange, then red and blue and yellow, one color per panel until her windows became a Rubik's Cube mural. No one could see in, but neither could she out. Unfazed, she hung a row of spider ferns from ceiling hooks and pushed her antique bed beneath the panes. The next day, she woke to the rosy glow of a church.

The storm passed overnight. Pale light leaks through the heavy brown curtains of my mother's spare room. Everything is still. I swing my legs over the iron bed frame and plant my feet on the hardwood floor. The air smells of mothballs and wood smoke, the smell of antique stores and adobe chapels, the smell of passing time. Glancing up, I stare into the face of the Virgin Mary, who stands before me on a pedestal, chalky white, arms raised, eyes downcast as if awaiting an apology. All around her, on every table, shelf, and wall of this room, stand saints and angels and altarpieces and crosses—restoration projects for my uncle, an artist-turned-priest who lived with us after my father died, and who stays here on his days off from his parish. He and my mother have been collecting these religious icons as they once collected Kachina dolls and retablos—to rescue them.

My eyes settle on three faded portraits of the holy family. In one, Joseph saws a heavy plank. Beside him, Mary, draped in pink and white, weaves a blue robe. At their feet, a young blond Christ raises a chisel to a wooden beam. Faces blank, they focus on their work, on their destinies. In the second, a white-scarfed Mary presents Joseph with a swaddled baby Jesus, who greets him unsmiling. Joseph leans forward with a basket of grapes and pomegranates, carpenter's ax on his shoulder. The third shows another child Jesus in a clearing. Rosy cheeks. Golden hair. Shouldering a heavy wooden cross. He gazes outside the frame—at the viewer. To his right, grape-vines. To his left, wheat. On a rock by his bare feet, three iron nails.

Everywhere symbols. Everywhere metaphors. Growing up, try-ing to understand my father's death, I looked to my mother for guidance. She showed me her faith most powerfully by healing stray animals, transforming scraps into art, seeing life in graveyards, and finding meaning in even the smallest of stones. It is that woman I have come to find—the woman who turned loss into love.

The curtains sigh in the breeze. I watch them rise and fall.

This used to be my room. My first room. At age sixteen, after a lifetime of sharing crowded quarters with my uncle and older brother, I moved into what had been my mother's sanctuary of ferns, Beatle albums, sketchbooks, and Chanel No. 5. When I took it over, I made it my own, replacing the jewel-painted windows with a laby-rinth design and playing my own records, *Toys in the Attic* and *Dark Side of the Moon*. I disappeared inside my own sketchpad and memo-rized every detail of this space—the hollow thud of the floorboards two steps from the door, the black crack of the closet that never shut, the ceiling-plaster continent shapes of places I longed to visit, Europe or South America, and the call of John Lennon's voice through cloth-covered speakers, "Imagine." Being here again feels as though I'm watching myself through my mother's two-sided, hope-chest mirror—everything familiar but nothing the same, lost in memo-ry's reflection.

A breeze drifts into the room. Mary watches me from her iron stand. I slip on my jeans and T-shirt and part the curtains.

As a boy I had a bad habit of banging my head and passing out. I'd sleep-walk to the bathroom, and stumble over the floor furnace, then smack my head on the doorknob. Or I'd chase my sister across the waxed hardwood floor, lose my balance, and catch the corner table behind my left ear. I'd have no memory of these accidents or the hours lost in darkness, but I'd open my eyes to my mother's voice and the bare bulb she'd wave like a lantern, guiding me awake.

So much green. I wander through my mother's backyard after the evening rain prepared to find a few branches scattered among the gardens of irises and fairy roses I remember so vividly, but confront instead a forest of overgrowth—chinaberry, catnip, silver leaf maple, crabgrass—choking away my past. The Russian olive tree once sweetening the air with lemony fragrance has toppled backward onto a coyote fence. The antiques once displayed like sculpture—potbelly stove, grinding wheel, hand pump—stand rusted and broken. The cement pond once used for pet ducks and geese has become a holding pit for branches. In the middle of it all, a child's wagon, axle busted, eaten away by rust. I grab a fistful of grass and pull. Straighten the wagon. Set it all right. Turn it all back.

"What are you doing?"

My mother appears behind me, eyes puffy from sleep, wearing a pale blue bathrobe. I stand too quickly and try to explain. The farther away I move from this house, the stronger its pull becomes, and the more I want to save what remains, to collect memories as she collects artifacts.

She searches my eyes the way she did when I was a boy, and after a minute, leads me by the hand to the northwest corner of her front yard, toward a bush as tall and wild as a forest troll.

"Pay attention. This is my quince. I transplanted her from my grandparents' ranch in Corrales. My grandfather always kept one hidden among his apricots and cherry orchards."

"Your grandfather?"

"Yes. Abenicio. He loved membrillos. During the holidays, he'd bring out a jar from the cellar, cut a slice of goat cheese, spread membrillos preserves on top, and drizzle it with honey."

"Membrillos?" I touch the thick waxy leaf. "What's it look like?"

"Brown. Sticky. Like figs."

"Any good?"

Her eyes widen. "Oh, the most exotic flavor you've ever tasted. Not like apples or pears. More subtle. More fragrant. My grandmother would add cloves or cinnamon sometimes. I used to keep a few in the fruit bowl on the kitchen table when you were little. Don't you remember?"

As soon as she said it, I did. "Yellow? Lumpy? Like pears only harder?"

"Exactly." Pinching my arm, she points toward a row of waist-high stalks with button-shaped buds. "These are hollyhocks. La vara de San Jose—staff of Saint Joseph. My grandmother had them all over the ranch. White. Scarlet. Pink. Lavender. I had lots of them, too. Remember?"

"Yes. Little ruffled flowers? Like little satellite dishes along the driveway. . ."

I survey the yard, but can't find what I seek. "Where's the lilac? Outside my old window?"

She touches her chest. "She collapsed when we installed city water a few years ago. We dug a trench under the window and she fell in, pobrecita. We transplanted her here."

She shuffles toward a stout bush with heart-shaped leaves and shakes it. "See how big she is? She's an old-fashioned lilac. Each year she gives me dozens of big lavender blossoms. Next to her is a French lilac. She's more bluish and more delicate. Not as fragrant, though."

I grip the branch like she does, squinting at the leaves to memorize every detail.

"Come over here," she says. "I want you to see this."

We duck beneath one of the pines along the driveway and head toward a shrub with fat oval leaves. "Here's my white lilac," she says. "I found her beside an adobe ruin near Galisteo. Imagine. In the middle of nowhere. A big, beautiful bush. I thought it was a miracle, so I brought a cutting."

I can see her doing it—straw hat and denim housedress, digging out the shoot with her irrigation shovel and wrapping it in an old T-shirt in her car trunk beside rocks and old boards.

"How many lilacs do you have?"

"I collect them," she says, yanking out a knot of crabgrass. "I used to have fourteen. But the jerk across the street poured something on two of them near the curb and they died."

She counts on her fingers.

"No. Wait. Including the backyard, sixteen. Yes. Sixteen."

Next, she leads me across the driveway to several semi-circles of pink granite.

"These are terraces. In my grandmother's day, no one had lawns, so they used these as planters. I'll fill them with mint, periwinkle, whatever. People think they're strange. But I like them."

When I pause for a closer look, she pulls me by the wrist toward an island of piñon trees and roses in the center of her driveway. She cups a small red blossom and angles it toward me.

"Smell that. Roses de Castilla. Aren't they fragrant? When I was a girl, all the Spanish houses had gardens like this. Roses. Irises. Tulips. Sunflowers. We planted early so we could have fresh flowers all year around. And for every season, we had a new blossom."

Laugh lines spread around her eyes. "Can I have a cutting?" I ask. "To take back with me?"

She reads my face. "We'll see."

Gathering her robe, she picks her way toward the side yard to unravel the garden hose. Honeybees swirl above her head, gold in the morning light.

Imperfect Blossoms

Dreams of. . . Roses

Her father builds for their family a house of river clay, thick brown blocks of Rio Grande terrón, cool in summer, warm in winter, cut from the valley itself. Carlos stacks the bricks tight, and stacks them again, as tight as his knitted fingers. Along the northern edge of the flat, sandy yard, as barriers from the llano wind, he plants Roses de Castilla, flowers of the Spanish missions, with small, dense, imperfect blossoms, less symmetrical than American Beauties, but with a votive candle fragrance he adores. My mother toddles behind him toward the thick, ruffled hedges carrying a chipped, white-enamel coffee cup filled to the brim with pump water. Carlos steadies her dimpled hands in his. Together, they pour.

This is her first memory.

. . . Treasure

She is not like her older sister and cousins, who hate visiting their grandparents' ranch while their mothers nurse the babies and their fathers head to work. The older ones whine when Adelida hands them baskets to gather breakfast eggs and complain when Abenicio asks them to churn butter. To the older ones, the ranch is work. Hard work. They would rather be with their friends in the city. Not my mother. She opens the barn door to a trove of steel tongs, silver spurs, iron rods, and brass bells. She descends the cellar steps to jewel-toned jars of cherries, plums, apricots, and honey. To her, the ranch is a mystery, a miracle, and each day when her chores are done, she explores the grounds with Abenicio's empty tobacco bags, gathering dandelions, rusty nails, prairie hawk feathers, and shards of aged blue glass. Treasure pouches, she calls them, and draws tight the yellow strings.

. . . Abenicio

She sits with her grandfather in the pink evening light while he savors his end-of-the-day cigarette. With scar-marbled fingers, he folds a tiny trough of Bugle brand paper, sprinkles in a sticky pinch of Golden Harvest tobacco, and quick as a coin trick, rolls a pencil-thin cylinder for his wind-burned lips. My mother hops up from the workbench and scrambles into the kitchen for a sliver of wood-stove kindling, returning a moment later cupping a birthday candle flame. Abenicio laughs his silent laugh, an earthquake in his broad denim shoulders, and chin held high, like Popeye with his pipe, aims his cigarette toward the lighted piñon twig. Abenicio drags deep, filling his lungs, holding it in for ten seconds, twenty seconds, before cooling the flame with a sigh. "Thank you, mi hijita," he says. His words rise on vaporous wings, and wreath his head of thick white hair.

. . . Adelida

On summer afternoons, when thunderclouds recede from the val-ley, my mother follows her grandmother from the ranch house to scrub-prickled llano, which glistens in the rain-washed light as if edged in silver. At the edge of an arroyo, Adelida bends to one knee to cup a budding yellow aster. "I call these my little jewels," she says, her own eyes a pair of agates. "They're all around, for us to enjoy, but we don't always pay attention. I wanted to show you this. So you'll remember." My mother leans forward to kiss the pinwheel face.

. . . All Things

On the ranch, when a shirt collar becomes worn, Adelida cuts it
away, turns it out, and sews it back into place. When a leather
rein snaps, Abenicio trims it, attaches a buckle, and fashions a
bridle strap. A truck tire becomes a tree swing, and a flour tin a
flowerpot. Nothing wasted. Nothing lost. All things rise anew.

. . . Empty Spaces

Gathering kindling one morning, my mother and her grand-father hear a mewling from the woodpile. Abenicio moves aside a piñon log to reveal a sickly orange kitten. My mother scoops it up, but Abenicio frowns. He does not need another hungry mouth to feed. Maybe it's better to let nature take its course, he says, but when my mother nuzzles the newborn to her cheek, he relents, so long as she cares for it herself, and promises to understand if it does not survive. My mother promises. That afternoon, she makes a nest of rags behind the chicken coop, and carries over a tin plate of cream. The kitten purrs and settles down to sleep. The next morn-ing, my mother returns to find the rags scattered and the saucer upturned. Coyotes, Abenicio says, placing a hand on her shoulder. The nature of things. Returning the rags to the barn, my mother pauses at a whimpering sound from beneath a worktable. Beside the legs of a stool, she discovers the watchdog, a yellow hound that had given birth to stillborn pups a few weeks before, nursing the bony kitten. At first, my mother is puzzled by the wondrous thing—the union of opposites, and how empty spaces can fill each other—but she remembers her grandfather's words. She fluffs the rags into a cushion. The nature of things.

. . . Lanterns

Abenicio doesn't believe in electricity. Doesn't want it. Doesn't need it. Believes it should be free of charge. Although utility lines stretch through Corrales, he prefers wood-burning stoves, beeswax candles, coal oil lamps, and kerosene lanterns, the old ways that have served him so well for so long. When my mother visits, he makes it her job to keep the lamps alight. She begins after breakfast, arranging the lanterns on the kitchen table into a kingdom of glass—fluted chimneys and crystal-cut reservoirs of amber, ruby, cobalt, and emerald. She rubs off soot with a kerosene-dipped cloth. Brushes away dead moths and mosquitoes. Turns the burner key three times clockwise to extend the wick, trims the seared edges, and turns the key twice counterclockwise. Unscrewing the reservoir cap, she steadies the funnel, refills the oil, and refastens the cap. Task complete, she glides through the shadows of the ranch house, carrying blossoms of light.

. . . Porcelain

From time to time, my mother is asked to pray at the bedsides of the sick and the dying, to offer the potent petitions of an innocent. At age six, she does as she's told, not frightened by these requests, not really. She believes in the words she recites in Latin. Besides, her grandmother always stands nearby. One evening, they are summoned to an uncle's ranch in La Ventana. When they arrive, my mother is told to wait outside the sick room while Adelida and two midwives attended a teenage cousin through a difficult childbirth. Again and again, the young woman screams, filling the hallway with cries so dark they might have been bats. My mother closes her eyes and begins to pray. After hours, after days, the door creaks open to wood smoke and lamplight. The old women emerge, faces hard as walnuts, and disappear down the corridor. From the kitchen, a grown man fades into sobs. My mother bites her lip, and steps forward to join them, but pauses at the sight of her cousin in the room—eyes open, unmoving, covered in red-soaked sheets, a newborn at her side, just as still, just as silent. How perfect he looks. A porcelain angel. My mother approaches the bed to touch his cheek. Cold. So cold. Gathering the bedding, she bundles his tiny feet.

. . . Veil

On Saturday evenings, she visits her great-grandmother, Preciliana, to help give the old woman a bath. When the sponging is done and Preciliana dries off with a towel, my mother combs her wintery hair. Tortoiseshell teeth pass through silvery strands like oars through water. A veil passes over Preciliana's eyes, a cloud across a reflecting pool, and my mother wonders, what does she see? Her boy's red rubber ball rising into the white summer sky? Her soft-handed husband climbing the front-porch steps with a bouquet of daisies? A hummingbird tapping window glass? Eyelashes flutter. Thin lips part. My mother smiles. She sees them, too.

. . . Urn

On hands and knees, she explores Preciliana's attic, sliding beneath the bare yellow bulb past hatboxes, perfume bottles, vanity mirrors, and gilded frames—toy box shapes in dust and shadow. She wants to touch one, to hold one, a pocket watch or a hatpin, to awaken the stories within. Before her, a golden round, a chalice or a cup, aglow in the amber light. She lifts the lacquered urn, the cherry-wood tobacco box carved by her great-grandfather, Pietro, who gazes down after death from a living room portrait, his autochrome eyes unmoving. My mother doesn't know him, doesn't remember him, but his smoke-scent she does. She opens the cracked dome lid to tobacco ash and matches. Rim to nose, she inhales.

. . . the Desert

She rides with apples and chile to the Dust Bowl ranchers of the Rio Puerco badlands, too small for heavy work, hugging produce barrels in the back of the buckboard wagon. Although she enjoys the stoic company of her grandfather and father, she comes instead for the desert—for the sundial shadows of yucca and mesquite, for the calendar turn of the wooden-spoke wheels, for the breathless wind that never stops talking, and for the cursive ripples on the heat-soaked sand, spelling the letters of her name.

. . . the Crossing

This much she fears—the Rio Puerco, the dirty river, the mud-brown tapeworm swallowing sheep and cattle whole. Abenicio and Carlos have seen it themselves, the underworld hunger, insatiable, but after decades traveling the llano, they have learned to read the sand. They approach the river on foot, probing with sticks, as if the ground might coil and strike. My mother cannot watch them. She hides in the truck bed and turns from the darkening edge, from ravine walls so high they blot the sun. Carlos lifts her to his chest. Carries her across.

. . . Gregorio

He drifts through the village like an autumn leaf. Once he was a respected attorney, pinstriped and proper, but when his wife leaves him for another man, he swallows rat poison and turns himself inside out, his eyes rolling back in his head. Afterward, he does everything opposite, waking at midnight, bathing fully clothed outdoors in the snow. Mostly he wanders, gazing from roadside weeds into lamp-lit windows in a moth-eaten suit, crooked bow-tie, and dusty bowler. My mother turns from her afternoon em-broidery and he is there, candle thin, range grass hair, staring into the sala through empty spectacles. She startles him, this pur-gatory soul, but meets his eyes with a smile. Gregorio tips his hat, shuffles away.

. . . Elias Tonto

Club-footed, claw-handed, toothless, and half-blind, he stands as
tall as a man but speaks as a boy, knocking on every village door
no matter the season to announce, "Merry Christmas," through a
rock-candy smile. Elias Tonto. Slow one. When he passes through
Corrales, crows trail behind him, and on winter nights, he sleeps
with Abenicio's cattle, hugging the beasts for warmth. When ranch
hands find him in the morning, dung on his clothes and straw in
his hair, Abenicio orders his sons to clean him up, and the boys,
it takes four to hold him down, haul Elias to the corral, strip his
clothes, and plop him in a washtub, scrubbing him pink with
horse-hair brushes. Once the bath is done, they wrap him in a
Navajo blanket, so tight so he can't lash out with fingernails and
fists, and sheer his sheepdog hair. Crying and screaming and asking
why, why, why, he wriggles his good hand free to paste back his
fallen curls. Old clothes burn with the trash. Sobs turn to laughter
when the boys return with denim jeans, a flannel shirt, leather
boots, and a wool jacket. Adelida hands my mother a basket of
apples, grapes, goat cheese, and tortillas. "Merry Christmas," Elias
tells her, and stumbles down the road.

. . . the Other Side

Late morning. Laundry day. Adelida changes bed sheets in the spare room and asks her fourth daughter, Balbina, and my mother, who is visiting again, to fetch spare blankets from a clothing trunk in the sala. The girls creak down a long hallway of mirrors and stop at a dark wooden door. Balbina twists the glass knob, but it won't open. She tries again. The handle spins in place. Shoulder against polished oak, she pushes. The door moves an inch, maybe two, but no more, as if someone is pushing back from the other side. Balbina thinks it's her older brothers, Benicio or Juan, and shouts for them to stop. No reply. She bangs on the door with her fists. Abenicio, interrupted by the commotion from his mid-morning coffee, barrels from the kitchen down the hallway. The door swings open before him. Abenicio looks left, then right, but the sala stands empty. He searches behind the settee, under the table, in the clothing trunks and behind the chairs, but finds nothing, no one. He checks the doors and windows, but finds them locked as well. On his belt, the only key. Adelida appears in the threshold and makes the sign of the cross. My mother bites her thumbnail. Abenicio closes the door behind them. Locks it tight.

. . . Rosewater

Pick fresh petals. Fill up your skirt. No stems or leaves. Come back into the kitchen and rinse out the bugs, and fill the saucepan with petals, but only a few inches deep. Pack them gently. Put water on the stove and wait until it's steaming, but not boiling. Good. Now pour the water over the petals until they're covered. Put the lid on the pan and let it steep until the water turns pink and the petals turn white and oil beads on the surface. Now strain the pan with a colander. Press down on the petals with a spoon. Good. Pour the juice in a jelly jar and you're done. This is rosewater, Adelida tells my mother. Splash some on your hands and face. Now you're clean.

. . . Harvest

They gather around a bonfire while Abenicio roasts onions, peppers, sweet corn, and chile. His sons strum corridos. His daughters harmonize. Wrapped Pueblo-style in wool blankets, Carlos sips apricot brandy and Desolina cinnamon tea. Embers rise like fireflies. Adelida rolls a campfire stone beneath my mother's boots. The warmth rises from her soles to her legs to her ribs through her bones.

. . . the Horizon

Autumn. Cedar smoke and apples. My mother sits with her grand-
father on the backyard workbench watching the sun flame out
behind the black gate horizon. Swallows streak across the orange
sky, as precise as ink quills on parchment paper. Abenicio leans
close. "You will never see this again. Not tomorrow. Not next week.
Not even two minutes from now. Look closely. It's already gone."

What They Will Do

As Carlos, my grandfather, aged into his seventies, my mother realized she didn't know him that well, not as a father, but as a man, as the person he had come to be. While Parkinson's stole his memory, she worried she might run out of time. He had always been a quiet man who said more with his hands than he did with his words. One winter morning, she sat at his kitchen table with a tape recorder she bought my brother for Christmas, switched the mic to "record," and asked him to tell her a story. Carlos arched his Cesar Romero eyebrows. Folded his arms. Said nothing.

She tried again several times afterward but with no luck. The tapes remained blank.

When spring arrived and snow melted up north she tried a different tack. She asked if he wanted to drive to Peñasco, where he had traveled in his youth. Carlos drummed his long fingers on the table. Nodded.

Once they hit the road in his powder blue F-150, he couldn't stop talking. His raspy voice crept up an octave. His lips curled into a smile. His Spanish crackled like chicharrones in a skillet. He seemed to know every village, church, and cattle trail in New Mexico. "That's where they used to plant wheat," he'd say, pointing toward a field near Casa Salazar. "And behind those apple trees," he'd say of Velarde, "they once grazed beautiful stallions."

My mother gathered his words like rocks from the mesa. With them, she assembled the mosaic of his life.

I drive with my mother through Corrales, hoping a tour of her birthplace will trigger her memories. We follow the main road into the village fifteen miles northwest of Albuquerque, hugging the meandering path of the Rio Grande, which flows glassy brown a hundred yards to the east behind thick stands of cottonwoods. Among the adobe homes plastered pink and white, I see glimpses of the alfalfa fields and chicken pens I remember from childhood. The morning sky glows apple green. The breeze carries traces of sweet grass and irrigated soil. I drink it all in, as rejuvenating as a tall glass of well water, but when I glance at my mother, she twists the purse strap in her lap, and stares out the window as if watching the end credits of her favorite Westerns, *The Searchers* or *High Noon*.

"This used to be corn," she says to herself. "All the way to the river."

"Still beautiful," I offer. "Isn't it?"

She shakes her head. "Not to me."

When I was growing up, we visited the village every month or so to buy bushel baskets of fresh fruit and green chile from produce stands along the road, but once her aunts and uncles sold off the family land, and newcomers began arriving from Texas and California, we stopped coming.

"The Corrales I knew doesn't even exist," she says, twisting the strap.

I know how she feels. I had said practically the same thing when I first arrived in Albuquerque and drove from the foothills to the valley down a road I had traveled a thousand times—a road that had always relaxed me as I descended from the subdivisions of the Heights to the farmland of the Rio Grande. Idling at the intersection of a sprawling office park, I took inventory of everything around me: Starbucks. McDonald's. 7-Eleven. Keva Juice. Wendy's. KFC. Home Depot. PetSmart. Office Max. Even worse, the intersection had been named, "Culture Boulevard," and the office park, "Renaissance." When the light changed, I couldn't drive away fast enough.

After circling Corrales a few times, my mother and I pause on the western border of the village outside a low-slung adobe home with pine vigas, picture windows, a covered porch, and a shaded courtyard—the house, I recognize from her stories and my own distant recollections, once belonging to her grandparents, Abenicio and Adelida. I lean over the dashboard to glimpse any detail I can of the rain barrels, rocking chairs, water pumps, and flower gardens she describes so vividly, but my vision is blocked by a four-foot-tall earthen wall and several leafy cottonwoods.

My mother shakes her head again. "It's not the same. Why do you want to see it?"

I want to match the place with the stories, I tell her, as she had with her own father. I want to overlay my memories with hers, like tracing paper over a photograph, to help them endure.

She sighs through her nose. "I'm getting tired. Maybe we should just go."

I wheel around the car to leave, but park at the last minute outside another squat adobe house just down the road from her grandparents—the house her father had built from river clay, the house where she was born. Once more I try to catch any image that might bring the origins of our family alive for me, but my view is again blocked by a stout wall and a leafy cottonwood.

"My father planted that," my mother says, peering at the gnarled old tree through her bifocals. "The one beside it, too. I used to climb them when I was a girl."

"Beautiful."

"No," she says, facing me. "You don't understand."

She points over my shoulder toward a field opposite the house —a long, narrow strip of knee-high weed-grass bordered by an irrigation ditch on the west and the main road on the east.

"All this used to be farmland," she says. "My grandfather owned it all. He planted fruit trees along the road, and in the middle, he planted alfalfa and hay. Way in the back, he grew squash and tomatoes and green chile and corn. By the little ditch, he had grapevines."

I follow her line of sight. "Are they still here?"

"Not like it was. My grandfather grew all kinds of apples. Rome Beauties. Winesaps. Golden Delicious. And peaches, too. Big, fuzzy white ones. Little yellow ones for canning. Plums. Pears. And the sweetest apricots you've ever tasted. For every season, he had a different fruit."

She sits up straight, eyes bright, and squeezes my forearm.

"Do you know what fruit they looked forward to the most? Manzanitas de San Juan—tiny yellowish-red apples. The sweetest, juiciest, most fragrant things you could imagine. My grandfather had only three trees, but he considered them delicacies. Even more than membrillos. They're very rare. They ripen only in late June. On the feast day of Saint John the Baptist."

She squints into the field. Points. "They used to be right there. In the center. Oh, I haven't had Manzanitas de San Juan in years. They're the best things you've ever tasted."

Excited by her excitement, sharing a memory with her at last, I throw a U-turn in the road and roll along the edge of the weedy field, scanning the few remaining trees for fruit.

My mother grabs my arm again. "Stop. That's them."

"What? Where?"

"Right there. Manzanitas de San Juan!"

She points to a withered trunk leaning sideways in the middle of the field. I flip off my sunglasses, but see only a few spindly branches and a scattering of shriveled brown apples.

"Really? Should I get some?"

She pinches me. "Yes!"

I kill the engine, step outside toward a barbed wire fence, and study the tree. All but two limbs have been sawed off. The remaining branches hold only a handful of sickly shoots.

"Looks dead. Or dying."

My mother places a hand on her chest. "I can't believe it. Manzanitas de San Juan."

Seeing her like that, I know what I have to do, but before stepping into the field, and onto private property, I glance down one side of the road, and then the other, acutely aware of the Colorado plates on my black Honda Civic and how outsiders are viewed in some villages. I give the portable trailer at the head of the field a long once over, half-expecting the owner to burst outside with a double-barrel shotgun, but instead see only bed sheets drawn down over the windows.

"Hurry," my mother says, head out the window. "Rescue them."

Holding my breath, I wriggle under the fence just as a faded red Chevy pickup rumbles by. A sunburned man in overalls scowls at me over the wheel, then taps his brakes as he passes.

I freeze, unable to decide which is worse—getting caught trespassing, or discovering that the apples have died, that there really is nothing left to save, that I'm chasing an illusion.

The truck rolls around the bend.

"Never mind," my mother says, waving me back. "I'll get them later."

I slide behind the wheel and look at her. She twists her purse strap and looks away.

We return to Albuquerque in silence.

"Manzanitas de San Juan," she says after awhile. "I wonder if that was really them."

Throughout my childhood, my family had a menagerie of pets: four mal-
lards, two Chinese ducks, two snow geese, a Toulouse goose, three German
shepherd crosses, a Labrador cross, five mix-breed cats, a Nubian goat, a
guinea hen, two peach-faced lovebirds, a peacock, a sparrow hawk, and a
screech owl. All strays. All adopted from the pound, brought home by my
brother, or carried to our doors by neighbors who knew we'd take them in.
After our father died, she wanted us to learn how to care for lost or wounded
creatures. And we did. Occasionally, though, despite her explicit instruc-
tions to check and double-check all the doors, windows, fences, and gates,
the pets went missing. Each night, she stood on our front porch as the street-
light flickered to life and called their names, hoping her singsong voice
would carry far enough to help them find their way. The next morning,
when she opened the screen door and the lost dog or lost cat sashayed in,
she smiled to herself, as if she expected it all along.

We stand in a graveyard. In the cemetery in Corrales. Knee-deep in the weeds, I hear a rustling—a lizard or a mouse, scurrying to my left, then my right, behind me or in front of me, just out of sight. I try to ignore it and focus on the task at hand, the reason I have brought my mother once more to the village—to find the missing graves of her aunt and uncle, Serafina and Pablito, who died long before she was born. But as I wander through the range grass and chamisal, where hardly a headstone remains, I'm distracted by the rasping sound, which practically calls to me.

"Are you sure they're here?" I ask my mother, who scans the brush beside me.

"Yes. I remember bringing flowers here with my grandmother. Near the entrance."

Hearing the fatigue in her voice, I feel bad again for bringing her here, this time to the century-old San Ysidro camposanto, a narrow rectangle of earthen mounds less than a mile from her grandfather's old house. After leaving behind what may or may not have been Manzanitas de San Juan, I had hoped to at least recover this part of her past, but we seem to be having even worse luck. There's little more to this section of the cemetery than Russian thistle and red ants. Still, I find it beautiful, so different from urban cemeteries with their hissing sprinklers and carpeted lawns. When I stand among those markers, laid as evenly as chess pieces, I feel next to nothing.

But here, with the faded flowers and rosary beads, I feel all the sorrow and love of the people who brought them. And yet, watching my mother step between the graves, hand to her chest, I can see how she might feel differently, how this might be difficult for her, confronting reminders of all she has lost.

Earlier in the day, I had taken her to Mount Calvary cemetery in Albuquerque to visit the graves of her grandmother, Adelida, and her aunt, Molly, who she loved as much as her parents. I scanned dozens of stone markers, ticking off names, Sanchez, Romero, Tafoya, and Matucci, before wondering aloud if I copied the wrong coordinates. When I looked to her for help, she just shook her head. She hadn't visited Molly's grave since the funeral decades earlier, she said. She hadn't visited her grandmother, either. When I asked why, she didn't answer. After an hour, I gave up.

I thought we'd have a better chance in the Corrales camposanto, which my mother does visit regularly. Before he died, she promised her father to tend the grave of her younger sister, Ernestina, whose weak heart failed when my mother was nine. Each Memorial Day, she pulls the weeds and waters the cactus she planted on her sister's dirt plot. During those visits, my mother finds that headstone instantly, as if guided. I thought we might discover Serafina's and Pablito's graves just as easily, but the longer we search, the greater my doubts. It's almost as if they're meant to stay hidden.

I close my eyes to summon a little intuition of my own, the way I do in the National Cemetery in Santa Fe where my father is buried. Whenever I visit him, I also find his headstone without looking. With only a vague sense of where I'm headed, I'll wander among rows of identical white markers and find myself gazing at his name as if I knew where it was all along.

Hearing the rustling again, I step toward the low stone fence near the entrance, where my mother remembered seeing the plots, but find only tumbleweeds. A moment later, I'm led to an anthill covered with broken glass. Finally, I stand before a tin nameplate covered in brush. I call my mother over, and we lean shoulder to shoulder toward the marker only to find it long ago erased.

She fans herself with her hat and moves away toward the shade of a cottonwood.

"I'll find them another time," she says over her shoulder.

I watch her a moment, unwilling to give up, and remain in the weeds, listening.

When I was a kid, my mother had a favorite blouse, a gauzy top of cream and sepia batik with a sundial design in the center. She loved how the pattern shifted like a Rorschach test when you stared at it—into a wagon wheel, or a hollyhock, or a pocket watch, or an eye. She liked the design so much she let us kids make our own, but instead of the wax-and-stain style of batik, she chose tie-dye. We drove to K-Mart and packed our cart with Fruit of the Loom T-shirts, rubber bands, and packets of Rit dye, which according to my mother had the most exotic colors—wine and tangerine and lemon and teal. Once home, she fetched the five-gallon water bucket we used for our pets, filled it to the brim, and placed it on our gas range, flame high. Next, she ripped open the shirt packages, used rubber bands to tie the white crew necks into knots, dropped them into the boiling water, and sprinkled in the powdered pigment. My siblings and I gathered around like witches, stirring the concoction with wooden pasta spoons and summoning spirits of steam. My uncle made a turquoise shirt with a crackle of purple lightning. My brother made a fireball of scarlet on yellow. I made a T-shirt of midnight blue with a blossom of white in the center that reminded me of the cottonwoods along the Rio Grande bosque, stepping from the shadows into the light.

The river has changed course, turning from the land as if recoiling on itself. Where the shallow brown current once hugged the bluffs above Corrales, it now arcs wide in the opposite direction, away from the bulldozers, earthmovers, construction signs, and terracotta roofs lining the horizon.

The sight of it stops me in my tracks, as if I have stepped onto the street of my old neighborhood in Albuquerque's North Valley and discovered a strip mall. My family and I spent countless afternoons on this bluff sliding down the slopes, sculpting faces in the sand, watching hawks ride the wind, and resetting our compass points of home. Seeing it now after decades away, a silence spreads through me as it had spread through my mother when we drove through her village.

"I hardly come here anymore," she says, folding her arms. "It's just not the same."

As if on cue, a man with a fanny pack and a pink Polo shirt releases a Labradoodle in the bushes below us to take a dump. Two joggers with orange Oakleys trudge past us toward a trailhead sign reading, "Made by Eagle Scouts." They nod at us. I nod at them. My mother turns away.

Kneeling, she examines a scattering of pebbles as if collecting the shards of a broken vase. I reflexively scan the ground myself, reaching down for a chamisal root twisting from the hill like a cottonwood in the moonlight. When I pull it toward me for a closer look, it begins to crack, so fragile it almost turns to dust. Startled, I leave it in place, and decide instead to slide down the sandy embankment toward the river, where I once dipped my hands in the cool brown water to relax.

Grasshoppers spring from the yellow grass. Hot dust fills the air. Arms wide to keep balance, I find my path blocked by a cottonwood leaning toward the ground like an old cowboy with a busted back—off balance, barely standing, but holding firm. A sign warns: "Keep Away. Unsteady." I stand beside the tree anyway and run my hand along the dry gray bark. In the cracks and creases I see the faces of my grandparents and great-grandparents and everyone else who once stood this ground. Looking up at the few remaining branches, I notice a few clusters of stubborn leaves.

My mother joins me. Smiles. "Amazing, isn't it? What they'll do to survive. See how it's twisted itself to reach the sun? They're very resilient, you know. Very strong."

Removing her sunhat, she picks her way through the rabbit bush and snakeweed to examine the trail again. Noticing me watching her, she says over her shoulder, "I'm looking for rocks. To make into worry stones. You should get something, too. To remember."

I glance back at the old cottonwood. In the sand at my feet, I see another broken chamisal root. I pick it up, dust it off, and slip it into my pocket.

Two

rescue |ˈreskyoō|

ORIGIN: Middle English: from Latin *excutere* 'to shake.'

verb [with obj.]
- to save (someone) from a difficult situation
- to keep from being lost

noun
- act of saving
- [as modifier] denoting excavation of sites threatened

verb
- to retrieve
- to free

Vessels

SHE DROVE into the desert after my father died, hour after hour along the asphalt arteries of northern New Mexico. She took no map. Had no destination. My mother relied instead, as she always had, on memory, curiosity, instinct, and faith, getting lost to find herself. She parked at the edge of the Rio Puerco badlands, one hundred miles from home, and stepped outside to face the wind. Head cocked as if she had heard her name, she smoothed back her chestnut hair, shielded her brown eyes from the noonday sun, and breathed in the aroma of sage and cholla and prickly pear and stone. Her shoulders relaxed. Her fingers opened at her sides. Her huarachas dug deep into the coarse blond sand. I stood beside her then, watching the worry lines fade from her face. Arms wide, I waited for the current.

Late morning, early summer. We were following a wagon trail near Cerrillos, gravel popping beneath the tires, heat rising from the hills, when we rolled up on a cluster of empty homes in a low valley split by a dry creek. In the rearview mirror I saw my mother smile. Our Comet slowed to a stop before an adobe with pink plaster peeling like a sunburn. She killed the engine. We stepped outside.

My big brother chased a blue-tailed lizard through the buffalo grass while my big sister slouched on the bumper and sighed. My middle sister knelt beside a budding blue aster and my little sister hugged her stuffed Thomasina, Cat of Three Lives. Me, I scanned the horizon of slump-shouldered boulders and tried to shake the feeling of being watched.

"I'll be back," my mother said, slipping off her sunglasses. "I want to look inside."

Nodding, my siblings stayed put, but I followed her, curious about her curiosity with this ghost town, as drawn as she was to an open doorway as black as the socket of a cow skull. Eyes adjusting from the midday sun, we stood in the threshold a few seconds until the shadows took shape inside—pine pole vigas caving in from a hole in the roof, a cast-iron stove sagging in a corner, a few broken chairs and overturned tables, busted beer bottles, pigeon feathers, and tin-plate ceiling tiles scattered on the floor like shaman bones.

"Be careful," my mother whispered, and slipped into the cool darkness, her denim silhouette enveloped, as if she had waded into a deep pond or passed behind a velvet curtain.

Holding my breath, I ducked inside, stepping where she stepped, Keds crunching through the breadcrumb stucco, fingers brushing wallpaper as brittle as autumn leaves, trusting that she knew the way. I found her in the center of the room stirring plaster shards with her finger, sliding them around like puzzle pieces as though assembling the history of this home and this forgotten village.

"Probably left during a drought and never came back," she said to herself as much as to me. "That happened sometimes in the old days. They didn't always have a choice."

She squinted into the cave-dark room, filling its emptiness with the swell of her imagination alone. I followed her line of sight, squinting like she did, hoping to summon the men, women, and children who once warmed these walls with candle-flame auras, but instead I saw only a swirl of dust and pollen in a shaft of pale blue light from the ceiling hole.

My brother called from outside. "I'm hungry."

Our mother stared into the vaporous glow.

He called again. "Mom!"

Blinking awake, she stepped toward the door, but paused before an old clothing trunk shoved against the wall. Reaching out, she passed her fingertips along the rotted canvas surface.

"My grandmother had one like this," she said. "When I was a little girl on the ranch they didn't have many closets so they stored everything in chests. Silverware. Sunday clothes. China. Linen. Sometimes, my grandmother let me play with her key ring—a big steel loop with dozens of keys—and I spent hours going through her trunks and all the beautiful things inside."

She creaked open the lid. "I called them my treasure boxes."

I traced the rusted keyhole with my thumb.

"Let's go," my brother shouted.

Sighing, our mother wiped her hands and stepped into the white sun.

I waited before joining her, peering into the trunk for what she'd seen, for what I envisioned she'd seen. In the water stains and cobwebs, I caught a glimpse: satin gloves, wedding lace.

On the back road to Cebolla, in a bristle-broom grass, we saw a large wooden cross—a splintering "t" leaning like a hitchhiker across a barbed-wire fence. We parked on the shoulder and fanned out across what turned out to be the half-hidden graves of an abandoned camposanto. My mother, as always, took the lead, squinting at the remaining headstones as if scanning the bookshelves of a lost archive, reciting names and dates as if they could reveal the mysteries of this long-dead place. Once again, I followed her, not so much afraid of ghosts as aware of their presence in the amber stillness of this late July afternoon. A hawk circled the clear sky. Dust rose from the snakeweed and thistle.

Halfway across the grounds my mother paused before one particular grave that seemed different to her than the rest: a small wooden marker with a heart cut from its center as neatly as if it had been scissored from a Valentine's card. She traced the contours of the negative space. A strand of hair fell across her cheek.

"A baby," she whispered. "Stillborn probably. That happened a lot back then. My grandmother used to help midwives in the country. Every family lost someone. But they endured."

I touched the design as she had and waited for her to say more —about a younger sister lost to rheumatic fever, an aunt killed in a train accident, an uncle who died as a boy from pneumonia, or even my father—but she just shook her head.

"See the date? 1901. And the name? It's worn away, pobrecita."

My mother had no family in this yellow valley 150 miles north-west of Albuquerque. No direct ties to this land. Yet she stood among the graves as if she did—head bowed, fingers knitted—as if her presence among the nameless dead might rekindle their spirits, if only for a moment. Raking her fingers through the hot sand, she extracted a stone of ochre and white, as dry as the bones of the llano. Nodding, she slipped it into the pocket of her blue jeans and walked ahead.

I sifted through the sand myself and selected a pebble as pitted gray as the weathered Valentine's marker. Holding it tight, I followed.

She loved photographs, fascinated since childhood at the notion of stopping time. Composition came naturally to her, as did lighting, framing, gesture, and mood, as if the portrait existed fully formed in her head. All she had to do was click the shutter.

My mother's favorite camera: a Brownie Bulls-Eye. Simple, durable, with a square body of heavy brown plastic, it fit snugly in her hands, and captured razor-sharp images through a hand-ground lens. Whenever she snapped a photo, a tiny lightning bolt flashed across the viewfinder.

She took her Brownie everywhere. No matter how high into the Pecos Wilderness we climbed or how far into the Rio Puerco Valley we drove, the brick-sized camera swung from her shoulder strap like a canteen. "Hold still," she'd tell me as I straddled a fallen pine on the high road to Truchas. "Say cheese." I hugged the log as if riding a stallion, transfixed by the flashbulb pop.

My mother rarely approached a subject directly, preferring instead to tilt the camera to the left or right, stepping back a few paces, holding the Brownie askew, and squinting through her viewfinder at a broken windmill or a bone-dry arroyo as though they were gallery installations.

Her photos were purposefully off-center—making the most of negative space, and angled just so to catch the golden slant of afternoon light or the spider-web pattern of a cracked door. It was as if she saw things no one else did, or was trying to adjust the world to match her perspective.

Always, she sought out the obscure, the overlooked, the abandoned, or the cast aside—a cottonwood hollowed out by prairie fire, a sunflower heavy with seeds, or a shepherd's shack crumbling into the stone hills from which it came. And everywhere, she saw metaphors—a cedar stump bent like a praying monk, a sunburst between the broken slats of a camposanto crib, or a white hand etched on the black face of an Anasazi petroglyph. In her eyes, everything held meaning.

One morning on the side road to Velarde she stopped on the shoulder to photograph an old iron bed dumped among the waist-high weeds. Kneeling in the orange dirt, she trained her lens on the diamond pattern of headboard rods with turquoise sky shining through rusty slates. When she finished, she handed me the Brownie and said, "You try." I steadied the camera with both hands, closing one eye like she did, and framed a strand of barbed wire curling through the sand like one of the morning glories in her yard. I clicked the shutter. Across the viewfinder, a bolt of lightning.

A Comet—a streak of 1967 peacock green metallic flake straight from the showroom floor to our driveway. Four doors. Streamlined chassis. Snow white hardtop. Small-block 289. My mother bought it after she traded in the Cadillac my father gave her when they were married—a silver 1957 Sedan de Ville. She barely had to tap the accelerator to leave her world behind. After my father died, it became too much for her to handle, so she handed the used-car salesman the keys.

The Comet was the first car she bought on her own. It took us places only a four-wheel drive should go—mesas, arroyos, escarpments, mountains—never breaking down or getting stuck.

That first day in our driveway, my sisters bounced on springy seats while my brother punched the chrome buttons on the dashboard radio. I sat in the gravel tracing the profile on the sunburst rims—the man with a winged cap and Roman nose, Mercury, messenger of the gods.

Sand the color of red chile powder covered the hills of our Jemez Mountain swimming hole, where we escaped the chlorine eyes of the North Valley elite and the RV tourists from Texas. Stepping from the Comet into the citrus sun, we entered a New Mexican Oz of turquoise, sage, juniper, and bone, drawn to a shimmer beneath stone cliffs and pine. I swam for hours with my Beatle bangs and Keds, although like my mother, I could not swim. While my big brother hiked trails cut by our grandfather during the Depression and my three sisters lay back on a broad blue boulder, I slipped into the snow-fed current. Goose bumps bloomed across my arms as I reached for wish-coin pebbles and fairy-swirls of light. I held my breath as long as I could before breaking to the surface like a rainbow trout—awake and alive. My mother sat back in the cottonwood shade with her slender white feet planted deep in the red-brown clay. In the black ovals of her sunglasses, a galaxy of stars.

We found the bluffs following an acequia to see where it led. Above cluster of cottonwoods some thirty feet from the Rio Grande, the dunes rose like a wave of white sand. Scrambling to the summit we found the four compass points of our home—the blue hump of

Sandia Crest to the east, the green swath of Bernalillo bosque to the north, the purple Stetson of Mount Taylor to the west, and the adobe rooftops of Corrales to the south. Standing there, my roots sank centuries.

My family visited the bluffs several times a month, scouring the mesa for fossils, gathering driftwood from sandbars, or eating picnic lunches in the sun. Often, I sat at the river's edge among the dragonflies and cattails, dipping my hands in the cool brown water to watch sunlight flash through the rosary bead droplets. In the current, I could hear whispers, words, even my name.

One afternoon my mother made a sand sculpture. On hands and knees, she shaped a nude woman on her back with her hair rippling down to her shoulders and her hands stretching out into the mesa and blending into the land. I made a boy's face. Rocks for eyes—round, green, open.

The church at Las Trampas stood at the foot of the Sangre de Cristo Mountains in a shallow green valley on the High Road to Taos. A stout rectangle of adobe and pine, San José de Gracia once served as a military outpost in Comanche territory on the northern border of New Spain. Dedicated to the Twelve Apostles, the two-hundred-and-fifty-year-old chapel rose on the backs of twelve village men into the shape of a cross, with massive walls, narrow windows, and bells in each tower—Gracia to mourn dead infants and the baritone Refugio for adults. The sanctuary had also been a morada for Los Hermanos Penitentes, who whipped themselves in devotion. Their bones, many believed, my mother believed, lay entombed beneath the floorboards near the threshold.

"They're buried right here," she whispered during one of our visits, making the sign of the cross before stepping inside. I hurried after her, leaving the bright summer heat for the cool darkness of the chapel, goose bumps breaking across my arms as we creaked past a tin basin bowl of holy water and a rickety stepladder to the choir loft. The air smelled of wood smoke and mothballs. Our steps echoed from the whitewashed adobe walls. On either side of us, along the narrow main aisle, stood two dozen mismatched pews with backs as hard and straight as the men and women who made them. Overhead, a herringbone pattern of latillas, vigas, and butcher-block buttresses. In the center of the twenty-foot ceiling, a wagon wheel chandelier with bare bulbs.

My mother padded silently ahead, sunhat in hand, swiveling left and right, memorizing every detail before stopping beneath framed portraits depicting The Stations of the Cross.

"Look at this," she said, waving me over to the image of Jesus falling for the third time. "See how expressive he is? Can you imagine the time it took to make this? The hard work? The sacrifice? The love? The people here are very devoted. You can see it all around."

I glanced over her shoulder as she spoke, trying to fill the pews with the leather-faced farmers and ranchers and vaqueros and fur trappers I conjured in my mind.

Next, she led me to the altar—a modest table draped with a white sheet holding white plastic carnations, votive candles, and a trio of two-foot santos adorned with satin gowns, hand-made lace, and delicate silver crowns. She pulled me close, inches from the gaunt wooden faces.

"Look at them. Just look at them."

Mary wore faded blue robes, her head low and her eyes downcast, as if absorbing generations of prayer and pain. Joseph leaned forward in a dark cloak, face blank, hands at his chest, as stiff as the pine from which he was carved. Jesus sagged on the cross, impossibly thin, impossibly white, hands too big, feet too big, head too big, almost puppet-like, blood pouring from gashes on his forehead, ribs, knuckles, and knees. But his eyes, his smoldering eyes, warmed me to the bone.

"He has real human hair," my mother whispered. "Do you see?"

I did. The places we visited and the things we saw were all vessels. And inside them, lives.

She sighed. Squeezed my hand.

Somewhere in the mountain forests near Chama, I wandered up a hill while my mother and siblings grilled campfire hot dogs in a meadow below. The air cooled as I climbed higher and leaves fluttered overhead like hypnotist coins. At the top of a rise I stopped to catch my breath and heard it—water or the wind, an insistent murmur, echoing all around me. I closed my eyes to listen as my mother had on the llano. All at once, a breeze passed over me, through me, and for a moment I felt part of everything—the rocks, the dirt, the pine needles, the black ants—dizzy with an electric tingle.

After awhile, I don't know how long, I snapped awake and stood there, noticing for the first time the bone-white trunks of aspens surrounding me, dozens of them, straight as prayer poles, lining the grassy peak. The hair prickled on my arms as if I had wandered onto a burial ground, and I felt suddenly, achingly, alone. My family didn't know where I was. I didn't know where I was. I had no boots. No jacket. No food. No water. Just Keds, cut-offs, tie-dye T-shirt, and a pocketknife. Steadying myself against the nearest tree, I felt on the pulpy bark a scar, rough and swollen, carved into the wood. With one finger I traced the blackened shape, which became initials—"R.C."—and then a date—"1911." Running my palm along the velvety trunk, I found more symbols—a rose, a heart, a woman's torso, a man's face, holes for eyes, a minus sign for a mouth.

Wind rustled the silvery leaves, the warm current tingling my fingers.

At that moment I knew what they were. My mother had told me. Shepherds. Alone near the Colorado border, they had left markings on aspens, like notes in bottles, messages to each other or anyone else who might pass, asking only: Remember.

My mother called out to me from the meadow below, her voice breaking the silence.

I turned from the tree to run, but hesitated. Slipping out the knife, I carved my name.

Three

root | root, roōot |

ORIGIN: Late Old English *rōt*, from Old Norse *rót*; related to Latin *radix*, also to *wort*. Old English *wrōtan*, of Germanic origin; related to Old English *wrōt* German *Rüssel* 'snout,' and Latin *rodere* 'gnaw.'

noun
1. the part attached to the ground to convey nourishment
2. the essential substance
   • ethnic or cultural origin
   • the fundamental note of a chord.
3. the value of an unknown quantity satisfying a given equation

verb [no obj.]
   • to search through a mass or area
   • to express the thorough or radical nature of a process
   • to dig or pull up
   • to find
   • to extract

PHRASAL VERBS
   • [informal] to hope for

noun
4. the part attaching to a greater more fundamental whole
   • the source

Origins

Dreams of. . . Los Corrales

First come the Tiguex, drawn to the slow brown river. In the black soil of the green bowl valley, they plant corn and beans, hunt antelope and pheasants, and thrive undisturbed for centuries. By the late 1600s conquistadores have pushed up from Mexico and claimed the valley for Spain. After decades of bloodshed with the Pueblo tribes, King Philip V offers a victorious corporal a gift in the new territory southwest of Santa Fe—106,000 acres of land from the mountains to the llano, long, thin parcels sliced like bacon for settling families named Sandoval, Gonzáles, Montoya, Chávez, Martínez, Candelaria, and Perea. Cattle graze. Alfalfa takes root. Horse stables rise along the western horizon. In the river lowlands, men point to the matchstick pens of the new out-post rancho and call it, "Los Corrales."

In the year of American independence, Fray Francisco A. Domin-guez scratches a quill across a parchment paper to record the Catholic missions in the territory of New Spain. In the budding village of Los Corrales he finds a settlement of two-parts, upper and lower, with thirty-six families, and an adobe chapel on the banks of a river called the Rio Grande. The village is served by priests from the nearby Sandia Mission and later Our Lady of

Sorrows in Bernalillo but the chapel itself, Dominguez notes, has no patron saint, no protector. This he writes in his book.

Storm clouds gather over the valley. In 1868 the Rio Grande swells, floods, and washes away the Los Corrales chapel and its tiny camposanto brick by brick. Coffins drift as far as Albuquerque. The village rebuilds. Workmen salvage rafters from the water, craft homes of river clay, rebury their dead, and raise a new chapel on higher ground in the shape of a cross. They choose as their patron, San Ysidro.

It is written: He is a humble man. Poor. Uneducated. Tilling the land of Tenth Century Madrid, Spain. Kind to animals and those in need, Ysidro dresses in hermit's rags and gives away his meager possessions to help the poor. Each and every day, regular as the rising sun, he celebrates Mass. In time, his fellow laborers become jealous of his virtues and his hard work among the crops. They complain to the master: Ysidro is always late. One day at dawn, horsewhip in hand, the yard boss set out to investigate and discovers Ysidro kneeling in the straw of a stable, hands clasped before him, eyes closed in prayer. In the fields, angels guide his plow.

In Los Corrales, spring arrives. Villagers carry a woodcarving of Ysidro through the rich brown furrows. Apples ripen. Alfalfa grows tall.

. . . Los Pereas

Los Pereas are traders, riding the Santa Fe Trail turning Mexican copper into gold. José Maria, patriarch of the Ojo de la Vaca clan, sends Abenicio, the eldest of his rough-hewn sons, seventy-five miles southwest to the family holdings in Los Corrales, and gives him a single charge: Produce.

Abenicio, pale green eyes, ash blond hair, more Basque than Spanish, squares his wide shoulders and smiles a peeled almond smile. He will do more than produce. He will become rich.

He is like his father this way—certain of himself. And there is this, as well. Everyone sees it: Abenicio is lucky.

. . . Abenicio

The storm catches him by surprise, though he dares it to come. Abenicio watches the thunderhead bearing down from Jemez Pueblo like an angry bull and thinks, as he has so many times before, that he'll simply dart away at the last moment like a charreada rider and cheat death one more time. Then the wind shifts, blocking his path with a blue curtain of rain, and he is trapped.

Abenicio leans into the muscled neck of his palomino and breathes in the sour mane. Gripping the reins with his right hand, he uses his left to gather his leather slicker around his shoulders, then pulls down the brim of a straw hat cured as hard as cottonwood bark. The wind slams into him. Hisses in his ears.

"One day your recklessness will get you killed. . ."

Alone on the Black Mesa, herding cattle and tracking strays, he often hears his father's voice, the sandpaper rasp of José Maria, pushing him, challenging him, redeeming through his sons some age-old sin.

"One day your luck will run out. . ."

Tired as he is, Abenicio can't help but smile. He has heard those words every day of his seventeen years. And his response is always the same: "We'll see."

The horse stumbles. Abenicio tightens his grip. Los Corrales stands some twenty-five miles to the south. He'll never make the rancho before dark.

He squints into the downpour. On a hillside thirty yards ahead, he sees the blur of a juniper, tent-like, with tough waxy needles. Dismounting, he lashes the reins to the branches, slips a shovel from his saddle, and begins digging a hollow beside the root ball. He unrolls two Navajo blankets, one for him and the other for the horse, which buries its head into the foliage.

Abenicio squats in the hollow, pulls the slicker over his hat, and fishes in his shirt pocket for the first of two cigarettes he rolled for the long ride home. Chin to his chest he lips the pencil-thin paper, sparks a match with his thumb, and inhales. The tobacco tastes good. Warms his belly. Closing his eyes, he drifts into a dream—riding into the badlands, silver heat and liquid sand, each hoof beat digging a grave, the llano shifting beneath him, seething. . .

He snaps awake.

The morning sky shines pink and green. Raindrops sparkle from the juniper branches like diamond earrings. His head pounds. He did not mean to sleep so long. Fumbling for the last cigarette, he fires it to life, takes a long drag, and stomps blood into his legs. Gathering the blanket from beneath the tree, he notices a lump beneath the wool in the hollow where he slept. When he nudges it with his boot, the lump moves. Tugging back the blanket, he freezes.

Rattlesnakes—writhing like worms. Drawn to the warmth of his body, they slept beneath him all night.

The horse jerks back its head, eyes wide.

Abenicio feels like he's sinking again. He reaches for the horse to steady himself and coughs. Tobacco smoke drifts toward the diamondbacks, which begin to move more slowly, languidly, as if drugged.

"Smoke makes them sleepy," says the voice in his head.

Abenicio takes another drag and breathes toward the juniper.

The rattlers become still and quiet.

Slowly, as if walking on glass, he leads the horse away.

Thirty yards from the tree, he puffs again to calm his nerves, but the cigarette has gone cold in his lips.

He laughs. No one will believe him. Then again, maybe they will.

Abenicio tips his hat to the juniper, and rides into the llano.

. . . Borderland

Abenicio builds his ranch on the outer rim of Los Corrales—on the borderland straddling east and west overlooking the white sandy hills of the west mesa llano and the loamy green swath along the Rio Grande. On this edge, between the pull of these two opposing forces, he raises livestock, scatters seeds.

. . . What He Sees

In the evenings, Abenicio sits outside against the sun-warmed adobe of the ranch house with his cigarette papers and tobacco pouch to savor the shifting sky. How he loves reading the moods of the valley. Clouds ablaze. The rising moon a currandera's eye. From his ranch, he sees the coming drought, the distant flood, the budding blossom, the early snow. From his ranch, he sees it all.

. . . What Passes Between Them

*Each spring, San Felipe de Neri church in Old Town Albuquerque
holds a fiesta. Everyone comes. Every man and woman for miles.
Abenicio snaps his pearl-button shirt and tells his younger brothers, Maximiliano and Juan, who have joined him in Los Corrales,
that he can't wait to see his fresh-faced "garden of roses." His
brothers laugh. Warn him of thorns. Abenicio slicks back his hair.
Ties his silver and turquoise bolo. He feels good. Lucky. At twenty-
two, people know his name.*

*In church before the dance, he notices a girl, barely fourteen,
with cascading auburn hair, creamy skin, doe-brown eyes, and a
white ruffled gown, gliding among the pews as a lily through pond
water.*

*A breeze blows through him, a feeling he once had as a boy,
when he awoke at the family ranch in Ojo de la Vaca and described
for his mother a vision he had seen in his sleep. "I know who I will
marry," he said. "I have seen her."*

*From across the adobe chapel, the young woman feels his
gaze.*

A century passes between them.

. . . Proposition

The night after the fiesta, when the people of Old Town open their doors to guests, Abenicio stands before the young woman's parents, hat in hand. He had introduced himself earlier in church, but the young woman's chaperone, an older cousin, glared at him with a face of stone. Still, he was persistent, some might say stubborn, and the two had danced throughout the night. Her name was Adelida, which sounded to him as beautiful as spring rain. Respectful of courting customs, he had sent her family a silver platter of grapes, cherries, apples, and figs from his orchards. Adelida's parents, Preciliana and Pietro, had politely accepted. But as they size him up now in his Western shirt, blue jeans, Stetson, and Colt .45, he can tell they regret their decision. Pietro scowls at Adelida, who sits beside him on the settee in the sala, studying her shoes. "What's your name?" Pietro asks.

Abenicio tells him.

Pietro, carpenter, merchant, farmer, strokes his waxed mustache.

He knows the Perea name.

Abenicio clears his throat. "I would like her hand in marriage."

Pietro laughs. His daughter, the oldest of three, is leaving in a few days. He has enrolled her in a Catholic school in his native

Italy to begin a formal education. She is, in fact, already packed and ready to go. "Thank you," he says, raising a finger. "But I must say no. Her life is not here. My word is final."

Abenicio nods, places his hat on the table, and calmly draws his Peacekeeper. "She wants to marry me," he says. "You can come to the wedding alive. Or dead. Either way, I am going to marry her."

Adelida watches him, cheeks aflame.

. . . Adelida

She brings to the ranch house Spanish roses, bone china, hand-blown Italian glass, and lemon-scented candles. When she sings arias in her crystalline soprano, Abenicio sets aside his hammer, hangs his hat on the fence post, and weeps.

Within the Walls

Dreams of. . . Refuge

Within the walls of his ranch house, Abenicio builds a hidden room. Narrow and windowless, it runs the length of the hallway as a refuge from bandits and war parties and whatever blows in with the llano wind. A dozen men, women, and children can fit inside if it comes to that, shoulder to shoulder, palms flat against the cool adobe. A single door allows entry—a false panel on a false shelf in the dining room. Lift an iron latch beneath a cupboard and release a sigh of dust and old wood. Along one side of the chamber, an array of shelves and nichos and boxes within boxes. Inside the boxes, land deeds and tintype photographs and old letters and jars of silver coins. Inside the room, secrets. Within the walls, stories.

. . . As Stone

She is alone with her infant daughter at their Ojo de la Vaca ranch. Her husband left at dawn to herd cattle near Santa Fe. As the sun ticks across the autumn sky, she slices steak for his suppertime return. The baby sleeps in a bassinet near the warmth of the wood-burning stove. The young woman hums.

A knock on the front door. A bang.

The watchdog growls from its backyard tether.

Another knock. Softer this time.

The woman sets down her paring knife, wipes her hands on her apron, and pads into the sala. Through gauzy curtains she sees a figure on her porch. Housedress. Matching bonnet. Turning from side to side as if confused or lost.

The young woman glances at her baby, checks her hair, and opens the door a crack. Eyes down, the visitor mumbles something about heading to Lucero to visit sick relatives. Walking all morning. Smelling the steak. Stopping to rest.

The dog barks in the backyard.

The young woman opens her mouth to say no, but the visitor cowers, almost as though crippled or injured, so she opens the door.

In the kitchen, the young woman resumes work. The visitor hunches at the table, face hidden beneath the bonnet, shrugging off small talk, silent as a stone. Strange, the woman thinks. Perhaps the visitor is shy. Or simple-minded.

Steak sizzles in the pan.

From time to time, the young woman feels the visitor's stare, but when she turns, the visitor looks away. Odd, she says to herself again. Something is not right. She studies the visitor once more: Housedress buttoned to the collar. Bonnet tied at the chin. Black leather boots. Riding boots. Men's boots.

The visitor looks up at her through rattlesnake eyes.

The young woman drops the knife on the counter and fumbles for it, making a joke of her clumsiness. Forcing a smile, she wipes her shaking hands on her apron, glances at the sleeping baby, and says she must fetch more firewood.

The visitor watches her. Nods.

The young woman steps from the kitchen into the yard with legs made of lead, and cuts the rope holding back the snarling watchdog, which shoots into the kitchen. Scrambling after it, the young woman sees through the doorway the visitor holding her baby before the open stove. He smiles at her. Tosses it inside.

The young woman screams. The dog knocks the visitor backward onto the kitchen table while she reaches into the stove to pull her daughter free. Blankets smolder. The baby vomits. The young woman's hands sting with burns.

The visitor staggers to his feet, face slick with blood, but the dog attacks again, and forces him down the back steps and into the yard.

The young woman holds her wailing baby. For an hour she stands there, unable to move, before willing herself to hitch the buckboard wagon and drive forty miles to a ranch house on the outer edge of Los Corrales.

The visitor fades into the llano, laughter alive on the wind.

. . . A Crack in the Sky

Smoke swirls into the kitchen, dark as malice. Abenicio doesn't notice. He sits on the floor playing with a red ant—pushing it into a gap in the hardwood, watching it scurry out, pushing it down again. His mother, Serafina, stands nearby frying chicharrones and choking back the greasy air. His stomach hurts. And has been hurting since he heard his mother and father whispering over their morning coffee about Navajo raids, bad blood, broken promises, dead ranchers, and revenge. The whispering made him nervous. Made him afraid. His mother is worried, too. He can tell by the way she scans the horizon when she opens the window to let in fresh air, then scans the horizon again. When she notices him watching her, she reaches down to hand him a tortilla stuffed with fried pork skins. Abenicio smiles. The bacon fat tastes good. Soothes his belly. The red ant scurries out again and he reaches out to sweep it back, but misses, and the creature scurries up the left leg of his overalls. He stands and stomps his pudgy sandaled feet.

A shadow crosses the floor.

Abenicio glances up toward the window at a face as sundried as deer jerky, with wet black eyes and iron gray hair tied back in a red bandanna.

"Can I have a tortilla, mamacita?"

The Navajo grins at them with glistening gums.

Serafina grabs the pan and flings hot grease at the window.

The scout screams so loud it hurts Abenicio's ears.

"Run," his mother tells him. "Run!"

Abenicio scrambles through the house, into the yard, and onto the buckboard wagon as fast as his four-year-old legs will carry him. His mother follows a moment later, hitching the horse, jumping inside, and snapping the reins.

The wagon bounces hard on the washboard road, so hard Abenicio thinks it will break, but they drive full speed to Arroyo Seco, where the men have been gathering barricade wood. Abenicio's mother scans the horizon again and again, but the Navajo seems to have taken flight on the wind.

At the arroyo, the men come running. Abenicio's father, José Maria, loads his musket while Serafina unhitches the horse and lifts Abenicio onto its back. Pressing a rosary into his palm, she tells him to follow the creek north to Santa Fe and get help. Not to stop. Not to look back.

Abenicio nods through tears.

His mother slaps the horse's rump and the beast leaps forward.

Abenicio's leg throbs where the ant has stung him, but he cannot, will not, release the reins. He will accept the pain for what he had done.

Cresting a hill, he glances over his shoulder to see his mother and father trudging up the arroyo toward the cover of trees. On the horizon, in place of their ranch, a plume of smoke, thin and black, a crack in the sky.

. . . Scars

There are no innocents on the llano. The sand is nourished with blood. José knows this. Tries to forget.

Spring of 1863: Kit Carson rides into Santa Fe seeking men who know the land like they know their women—every curve, every scar. Carson, who has beaten back Texas Confederates south of Albuquerque, has new orders. Handle the Navajo and Apache. Shoot men on sight. Take women and children prisoner.

José Maria knows the land. He speaks Navajo and Apache, too. Although he doesn't trust gringos, never trusts gringos, he signs up as a scout. He'll ride with the soldiers. He'll watch the hogans burn. He'll cleanse the haunting memories of open graves and thick black smoke and swirling ravens and war party cries. He'll take the Yankee's gold and use them as they use him.

That summer, José Maria sets out tracking a few straggling raiders in the rawboned hills near Magdalena. Early one morning he approaches a cave and hears voices within. He sets aside his musket and chooses a lance he had taken from an Apache captive on an earlier mission. He has always admired the Apache lance. Elegant. Noiseless. Deadly. He practices for months learning how to use it.

José Maria counts to ten. The lance sails into the crevasse.

Grabbing his musket, he orders everyone outside—in Spanish, Navajo, and Apache. After a long silence, a Navajo woman limps into the slanting sunlight, the lance piercing her right thigh. She is young, as young as his own wife. A boy and a girl, no older than four, follow her outside.

José Maria stares down his barrel, but the woman stands firm, breathing hard through flared nostrils. He orders her to kneel, to tell him where the others are hiding, but the woman and her children just watch him, eyes like embers. He cocks the musket. Blood pools at her feet. Her eyes roll back in her head, and she faints.

He moves without thinking, setting aside the gun, pulling the lance from the woman's leg, and cinching her thigh with the belt. With lasso rope, he lashes together a travois from branches of mesquite and piñon and rolls her onto it. The children watch him, unmoving. In their eyes, he sees his younger self, standing before rows of open Spanish graves, smoke and raven's wings swirling away on the wind.

José Maria leads his captives toward a forced-march convoy headed to Bosque Redondo one hundred miles east—The Long Walk of the Navajo, New Mexico's own Trail of Tears. He collects his bounty and rides to Ojo de la Vaca.

The sky burns red as he arrives. His horse trembles. Wordless, he walks into the llano and sets alight a pile of dry brush. Stripping his bloody clothes, he tosses them into the fire with the lance, then stands alone, naked before the flames.

Sorrowful Mysteries

Dreams of. . . Sanctuary

At the end of the ranch house hallway stands a door with a blue glass knob. Only Adelida holds the key. Behind the door, a closet chapel. Inside the chapel, a small wooden kneeler and a small wooden table. On the table, beneath a painting of The Sacred Heart, the family saints: San Juan Nepomuceno, protector of bridges and secrets; San Miguel, defender of the righteous, the weigher of souls; Santa Lucia, a guide to the blind, and a giver of light; San Antonio, finder of lost things, and protector against storms; Santo Niño de Atocha, patron of prisoners and afflicted children. Adelida visits once a day, often twice, to pray for her children: Desolina, Benicio, Pablito, Serafina, hour after hour, the sorrowful mysteries. With her thumb and forefinger she rubs the olive wood beads, which drink in her sweat and oil and hope and fear, deep as memory, thirsty as bone.

. . . the Looking Glass

Mirrors line the ranch house walls. Frames of all shapes and sizes bending light to the darkest corners. The hallway alone holds a dozen glassy portals on either side. Whoever walks the narrow passage from the kitchen to the sala has the sense of being accompanied by other selves, twin spirits on the left and right, guiding them from door to door. In the sala hangs the most elaborate looking glass—a three-foot Florentine import with gilded mahogany edges and a beveled surface as clear as water. Adelida stands before it each evening pulling a tortoiseshell comb through her thick auburn hair, each stroke an oar in the river of dreams. Desolina leans in the threshold watching her mother's eyes, wondering what they behold. Whenever she gazes into the silvery surface, Desolina sees only pale skin, freckles, rusty hair, and old wood. She feels only the emptiness of watching nighthawks slice across the llano sky, wishing she could fly that fast, that far.

One morning while her parents work in the yard, Desolina decides to show her pet bull the sala mirror to see what will happen. Looping a rope around its muscled black neck, she tugs the torito inside the corridor. The beast moans, spooked by the flashes of light and shadow, so Desolina pulls harder, dragging its hooves along on the floor. In the sala, she steadies the animal's head before the gilded frame. The bull stares into the mirror, wet black eyes on wet black eyes, lowers its head, and charges. Shards spray through the dusty light. The bull scrambles back down the hallway, through the kitchen, and into the yard.

Desolina sits unmoving, cheeks wet, gazing into the blackened oval.

. . . Echoes

Late one night after an autumn dance in Alameda, Benicio heads home to the ranch house along an acequia near Bernalillo, drunk on red wine, cheeks hot from the slaps he has collected with stolen kisses. Despite Adelida's warnings, he takes a shortcut to Los Corrales through the Rio Grande bosque, where bats and black widows dwell. Benicio shrugs it off. He fears nothing and no one, not even the moonless sky. Stumbling down the ditch bank to piss, he sees a young woman in the bushes, her face covered, whimpering. His first thought—another kiss, maybe more. He calls out to her. "What are you doing? Hiding from me?"

The woman begins to sob.

Benicio laughs. "Come on out. I won't bite."

Parting the branches, he steps toward the woman, whose head and shoulders are hidden beneath a black lace mantilla. As he reaches to embrace her, she parts her veil. A skull grins at him— bright as the emerging moon.

Benicio runs. Like a wild horse he runs. The woman flies after him with owl's wings, cackling as he scrambles up the acequia walls. Three times she swoops down with black talons. Three times he beats her back with bloody fists.

After hours, after days, he reaches the ranch house, and claws at the front door. Adelida meets him in the threshold with a lantern

*held high, a white sword of flame. Before he rolls inside, Benicio
wheels around to face his demon. In its place, he finds only the
rustle of leaves, the scent of smoke, the echo of laughter.*

. . . an Aria

*Pablito is different. Everyone sees it. Sabio, they call him. Learned.
By age two, he speaks in full sentences, in Spanish and English,
each word enunciated with the clipped tones of a priest. "Listen.
I have something to tell you."*

*In appearance, Pablito, eighth of fourteen children, resem-
bles his father, Abenicio, with the candle-flame hair and olive
skin of the Pereas, but in temperament, he is his mother's son, a
Paladini, sharing her love of roses, linen, sautéed garlic, and Italian opera. They spend hours together, her singing arias, and him
combing her hair. He is peculiar, though. Everyone sees this, too.
He never addresses his father directly, but speaks instead through
his mother, whom he calls by first name. "Adelida," he'll say at the
kitchen table, hands folded like little birds. "Tell your husband to
fetch the cows from the mesa. It is going to rain. Their hooves will
rot with fungus and they will die. Tell him to bring them home."*

*Abenicio will sip his coffee and shake his head. But the cows
will develop a fungus. And they will die. And his family will learn
to listen.*

*One damp spring morning, Pablito shuffles into the kitchen
while his mother feeds kindling into the wood-burning stove. He
stands patiently while she works, hands in his trousers pockets,
until she faces him. "I am very sick," he tells her. "Have one of your
sons fetch your husband from the mesa. Tell him to take me to
Albuquerque—to Old Town. I need to see a doctor. And very soon."*

His mother places her palm on his eight-year-old forehead. Peers down his throat. Listens to his heart. He looks fine. Tired, but fine.

"I'm sorry," she tells him, checking his ears. "Your father is very busy. He's branding the cattle. Maybe you just need to rest."

Pablito tugs her apron. "Please. Tell your husband to come home now. I am very ill. If you don't do this, you will be sorry the rest of your life."

Adelida looks into his pale green eyes, as clear and deep as a pond. Nodding, she orders Benicio to saddle up his horse and relay the message.

On the llano, Abenicio staggers back from the branding fire, pulling off his leather gloves with his teeth. "No. I have to finish. I'll be home before supper."

By late afternoon, Pablito's breathing becomes shallow. His face becomes candle wax. Adelida strips his nightshirt, mops his forehead, and spoons him chicken broth and yerba manzanilla tea. Still he burns. His hands melt in hers.

At sunset, Abenicio finally arrives. He takes one look in the sick room, scoops up Pablito, and loads him into the wagon. Pablito sleeps open-eyed in Adelida's arms, gazing behind her, beyond her, at a place she cannot yet see.

In Old Town, the doctor clicks shut his bag and ushers Adelida into the hallway of her mother's home. The doctor cannot help him. The fever is too high. The pneumonia is too advanced. There is nothing to do but pray.

Adelida kneels at his bedside the entire night, below a portrait of Jesus Christ in white flowing robes, his pink heart exposed, his chest alight.

"Why did you not listen?" Pablito says. "Now you have lost your boy."

He turns from her and faces the portrait, eyes fixed upon the flame.

. . . Justino

*He blows in from the badlands with the shimmering heat, a dust
devil with a Colt .45, a specter of black leather and Mexican
silver conchos. Justino Mirabal. Name like Justice. Desolina watches
him from the ranch house porch behind Abenicio, more curious
than afraid. She knows the name. Hears the stories—Justino,
avenging angel, Robin Hood with a Zapata mustache, killer of
blue-eyed men who carve into the New Mexican territory like so
many porterhouse steaks. But no matter how many deputies saddle up or how long they scour the yellow hills above Cubero, they
can never pull Justino from the llano's embrace.*

*Abenicio steps forward to greet his nephew, arms wide. As a
boy, Abenicio attended boarding school in Chihuahua, and worked
the land with the sons and daughters of La Revolución. Whenever
Justino's black stallion straggles up to his trough, Abenicio gives
him blankets, coins, dried beef, and bullets.*

*Justino dismounts, ties his horse, and flashes cool green eyes at
Desolina, who sees a shimmer she recognizes. Startled, she scrambles
into the sala, down the hallway, and beneath the kitchen table to
hide. A moment later, she hears riding boots thud up the steps, down
the corridor of mirrors, and into the kitchen. The boots stop inches
away from the table, spurs jingling, sharp as the evening star.*

*A sandpaper voice:"Where are your daughters? My beautiful
flowers?"*

Her father's laugh: "Hiding from you, hombre."

The squeak of a cork. The tinkle of shot glasses.

Abenicio speaks through clenched teeth about Mormons slaughtering Spanish sheep near the Arizona border. Carcasses piled high. Left to rot.

Justino spits. His saliva sizzles on the dry pine floor.

Desolina bites her knuckle.

"Salúd," Justino says. "Now, how about those bullets?"

The right boot turns on its heel, its spur sinking into the wooden planks, before thudding down the hallway and onto the front porch.

Desolina counts to ten and crawls out.

On the table, she notices a glass holding a trace of silvery liquor. She picks it up and drinks. The tequila tastes good, hot as anger. She licks her lips.

Kneeling, she touches with her fingertips the floor where Justino's spur has sunken into the pine. His mark is deep, round, permanent.

. . . the Stand

When the wind rages and thunderheads bruise the sky, Adelida
unlocks her closet chapel to retrieve her bulto of San Antonio de
Padua. She stands on her front porch step and holds high the
unblinking saint. Lightning flashes. The llano screams. Water drips
from her fingers.

. . . Blossom

*Serafina sings like a meadowlark. Hand her a ribbon, she will
sew you a rose.*

*One summer at a cousin's baptismal gathering near Gallina,
the children play outside when a dog straggles from the llano, teeth
bared, coming at them erratically, chasing one, then the other.
Everyone runs, but Serafina, dressed in a dress, cannot move fast
enough. The dog, a blur of black, bites her leg.*

*Adelida attends the wound. Not too deep. Not too dirty.
Perhaps her oldest daughter will heal. Then this: Serafina sits at
home in sala embroidering vines on a handkerchief when a cloud
darkens the sun. Her eyes roll in her head. Her fingers curl into
claws. Even Abenicio cannot hold her down. Adelida brews her
altamisa tea, rubs her temples with piñon ash, bathes her fevered
limbs in a tub of rose water, and still Serafina swims in a night-
mare of teeth and shadow.*

*Alone in her chapel, Adelida prays to Santo Nino de Atocha,
patron of pilgrims, prisoners and afflicted children, whose carved
likeness graces the altar at Santuario de Chimayo, one hundred
miles north of Los Corrales. If the Child Christ will remove the
sickness, Adelida implores, Serafina has promised to sew him a
new hat, new cape, new gown, new shoes. She will offer what gifts
she has.*

Abenicio readies the wagon. Once more the fever returns. Once more darkness swirls. When Serafina awakens, she takes up her needle and thread, and from her fingers rise bouquets of silk and satin and lace.

At Santuario, mother and daughter dress anew the wooden saint. They comb locks of real human hair, slip new leather over well-worn feet, and gaze into eyes of porcelain and blue. Shadows tremble. Beeswax crackles.

On the breeze, the scent of roses.

. . . the Pulse

On the south side of the ranch house, in the clear, clean after-
noon light, Abenicio grows pomegranates—fruit of the Spanish
missions. Once a day, often twice, he holds the sanguine flesh, and
rubs with callused fingers the smooth, ruby skin. For his children,
his wife, his sins, and his graces, he nurtures the tree of hearts.

Four

trespass | ˈtrespəs, -ˌpas |

ORIGIN: Middle English: from Old French *trespasser* 'pass over, trespass,' *trespas* 'passing across,' from medieval Latin *transpassare* (see trans-pass).

verb [no obj.]

1. enter without permission:
   • make unfair claims on or take advantage of
2. (archaic or literary) commit offense
3. infringe on privacy, or time

noun

1. an intrusion
2. a sin

synonyms:
   • fall from grace:

   "He asked forgiveness for his trespasses"

Gesture

WE STAND again among graves, dozens of yellow-brown head-stones scattered like broken teeth in an abandoned camposanto near Cubero, some sixty miles west of Albuquerque. My mother wants to show me why she travels into the desert to collect artifacts—and for whom. She enters the grounds first, as she always does, blending into the sand and scrub with her olive housedress and sun-streaked auburn hair. A plastic bag rattles from a juniper. A hawk glides across the milky sky.

I feel a sudden chill. And I'm not sure why. I've visited cemeteries all my life with my mother and never once been afraid, but here, I sense a foreboding or malice lingering like the gauzy clouds. The camposanto itself is hardly imposing. It's little more than a rectangle of headstones and weeds about the size of a strip mall parking lot. The graves themselves are mostly yellow dirt and rust-colored rock. When I join my mother and describe the odd sensation, she frowns.

"Really? I think it's beautiful."

She has been visiting the cemetery for years. Her mother's cousin, Justino Mirábal—the Robin Hood vaquero—hid out in these hills from frontier lawmen.

"They could never find him," she says, grinning. "There are secret caves all around."

I follow her eyes along a rocky horizon so riddled with holes and crevasses it could be a giant slab of termite-infested driftwood. Looking deeper into the creases and folds, I can almost see hooded figures and empty faces. I feel the chill again and rub the goose bumps from my arms.

"That's not why I brought you here," my mother says, watching me. "Look."

She touches a sandstone marker at our feet etched with flowers and religious symbols.

"See the craftsmanship? The Spanish-Moorish cross? The name?"

I squint at an inscription curling across the pitted surface as gracefully as the decorative vines around it—*Fulgencia Tafoya-Nacio Agusto 1902 / Murio Feb. 14, 1903*.

"A baby?"

"Yes," my mother says, lowering her voice. "Do you see how it's been ruined?"

She smoothes a pea-sized crater above the name.

"A bullet hole."

I touch the blemish myself. It does seem too deep, too smooth, and too symmetrical to have been made by wind or rain or normal erosion.

"They're all like that," she says, frowning again. "Go see for yourself."

I wander off on my own. After only a few steps, I see she's right. All around, markers have been tipped over, broken in half, or busted to pieces as if vandals ran wild with sledgehammers. I pass a smashed infant's crib, an angel with its face cracked, and a shallow grave filled with empty Jack Daniels bottles and porno magazines. Stepping around the hole, I stumble over the severed head of a pit bull, its yellow teeth bared, its pink flesh glistening beneath matted brown fur.

My mother stands beside me and makes the sign of the cross. "Desecration."

A year earlier, she explains, she and my uncle, the priest, had visited the cemetery and found dozens of broken statues: Saints. Angels. The Virgin Mary. Little children. She had wanted to take them home and repair them and bring them back, but my uncle told her to let them rest in peace.

"Now, I wish I had rescued them," she says, looking away. "Because they're gone."

I lean toward a fallen marker engraved with the profile of a young girl praying. When I try to push it upright, my mother touches my shoulder.

"Leave her be. She's been disturbed enough."

I survey the hills again. The holes. The faces.

"Who would do this? Why?"

She shakes her head. Drunks. Bikers. Tweakers. Bored teenagers. Black market art thieves. Angry activists from one of the nearby pueblos who resent the Spanish as much as the Spanish resent the Anglos. Maybe even one of the cults or covens rumored to roam these hills.

"Doesn't matter," she says. "I just wanted you to see."

Staring down at the headstone, I do see. This past—her past— is fading, if not being outright destroyed. Still, I wonder if my uncle is right. Maybe the best way to honor these people is not only to cherish the artifacts, but the gestures behind them, the acts of love and remembrance.

My mother whispers a prayer.

After a moment, she leads me out through the graves.

Prayer for Rain

HEAT RISES from the highway, shimmering between the rolling hills like puddles of air. Ahead on the horizon, a brood of thunderclouds. My uncle raises a finger from the wheel and says, "Really coming down. And just where we're headed." In the back, my mother whispers, "Jesus, Mary, and Joseph. Take this storm from our path." Mid-morning. Late summer. Our journey has just begun.

I settle into the shotgun seat and stare into the vanishing point of Interstate 40 and Mount Taylor west of Albuquerque to conjure an image of our destination—Marquez, mythic Marquez, the yellow stone village where my grandfather, Carlos, once found sanctuary as a boy after running away from a boarding school in Santa Fe. I heard the story so often growing up it practically has become my own. When my mother tells it I can see myself crossing mile after mile of hot sand, then bedding down in a cool, dark cave where a mural of the Virgin Mary watched over me. I have asked to visit the village to reconnect with that history—to walk that ground again, to make it real.

We're not prepared for the badlands. Not really. My uncle, my mother's youngest brother, has taken a day off from his parish near Taos to be our driver. He wears black slacks, a black crew neck, and black athletic shoes, as stoic as one of the wooden saints in his church.

My mother, the third oldest of eight children, wears her usual straw sunhat, oversized sunglasses, housedress, and gardening boots. Me, I'm even more out of place in my cargo shorts, Denver Nuggets T-shirt, and cross-trainers. We have no canteens. No compass. No map. Once again, we follow memory.

"Looks bad," I say, pointing toward the storm clouds. "Maybe we should turn back."

"Why?" My uncle scowls. "We'll be fine." He glances at my mother, who makes the sign of the cross. Nodding, he reaches toward the rearview mirror and a strand of pale blue rosary beads.

❧

An hour into the drive we leave behind the blur of semi-trucks and RVs and turn north at Laguna Pueblo onto a narrow gravel road unwinding toward Marquez like an endless rope pulling us past Paguate, Moquino, Bibo, and Seyboyeta, village names I have never heard, village names that stick in my mouth like cactus candy. Drowsy from the heat, we stare through open windows at buckskin plains speckled with gray tufts of chamisal, yellow splashes of range grass, mossy sprigs of piñon, and black fingers of cholla. The farther we drive, the sharper the colors become and the more pronounced the contrasts. Every contour is heightened by the summer sun. Every blade of grass is twisted toward water or shade, shaped by this unforgiving land, yet somehow enduring. In a swirl of dust, I see the khaki silhouette of my young grandfather straggling over the charred escarpment, lanky and sunburned, an apparition of rags pushing through hell toward a liquid vision of home. I feel that pull myself—firm ground, roots, a resting place.

"I wonder how he survived," I hear myself saying. "Out here in this."

My mother touches my shoulder. "His friend knew the way. He was from Marquez but went to Santa Fe to learn how to read and write. Farmers and ranchers did that in those days—sent kids to boarding school during the off-season. His friend got homesick and took Granddad with him."

My uncle nods. "They made it all that way by themselves."

"But how?" I ask. "A hundred and fifty miles? On foot?"

"They followed the Rio Puerco as long as they could, then turned west toward Mount Taylor. They ate the jerky and hard cheese they'd packed and then picked apples and piñon along the way. They slept in barns and shepherds' shacks during the day and traveled at night. They drank from streams or rivers. They lived off the land like they'd been taught. Why? Don't you believe me?"

I do believe, I say. Always have. The stories are beautiful. From them I draw a sense of who I am. The people and places she describes are alive inside me, fully formed, as if I've always known them. When she speaks, she awakens a dream. I'm just trying to align what I feel with what I see.

"What happened was a miracle," she says, removing her hand. "You don't understand."

We drive in silence. Gravel pops beneath the tires.

My uncle steers past a hillside of gray chunky rock. Under the bare-bulb sun, a shape takes form on the summit—a stone shack, square as a helmet, leaning forward from its dusty camouflage. Through the empty windows of the shelter I see two rectangles of turquoise sky.

"He probably stayed there," my mother says, pinching my arm. "Told you it was true."

I never doubted her, I say. I only want to see more clearly. She turns away.

A few miles from the shack, we pass what appears to be an arroyo, but as we pull closer, becomes a ravine, then a canyon so deep it looks as if the ground split open during an earthquake.

We park the car. My mother grips my shoulder as I approach the edge.

"Not too close. There are sinkholes all around. You could fall in."

"She's right," my uncle says, scanning the ground. "Looks can be deceiving."

I stare down into the canyon for the water keeping this land alive, but see only the thinnest ribbon of silver, barely a flicker, there and gone.

From the horizon, thunder rumbles. We hurry to the car and leave.

Approaching the blue hump of Mount Taylor, the landscape changes again—from yellow-brown to chalky white, as if the llano has been dusted with ash. Sharp-edged boulders dot the hills.

My mother reaches over from the back seat to touch my uncle's shoulder. "Remember my horseshoe? Aren't we close to where I found it? By those rocks up ahead?"

Nodding, he points over the dashboard toward a small pile of stones off the shoulder to our right, a few dozen yards east of us. "Good memory. Right up there. Just a little farther."

A year earlier, the two of them had visited Marquez for the first time in several years. Instead of traveling in the summer heat as they usually did, they drove in the early spring to see the daisies and asters blooming among the buffalo grass and sage. Creeping along the gravel road, my mother noticed a thin black shape twisting up through the stones. My uncle parked on the roadside. The shape wasn't moving, so they stepped outside on tiptoes, wary of stirring rattlesnakes from hibernation. As she approached, my mother slipped on her bifocals, and pulled free a rusty horseshoe bent into an "S." In a rocky cove above it, she found a hand-painted name, "Eliseo Marquez," which she recognized from her father's stories as one of the families that had taken him in. The artifact had been kicked loose by a horse, unearthed by a road grader, or placed as a marker by family members. Whatever its purpose my mother took it as a sign she was meant to return.

"I don't know how she saw it," my uncle says, laughing. "With all that rock and cactus? And with her eyesight? It was a miracle."

"Yes," my mother says, eyes wide. "For some reason I was meant to find it."

My uncle hits the brakes. "There! Right there."

Following his light of sight, I see it, too: "Eliseo Marquez," painted black on white stone.

My uncle nods. My mother makes the sign of a cross.

"Quite a coincidence," I say, slipping off my sunglasses.

"No," my mother says. "He must have died there. Or passed through this road. His family wanted us to see him. To pray for him. There are restless souls all around."

My uncle whispers a prayer.

I stare at the name. It shimmers in the heat, almost alive.

The road takes an eastward turn from the purple clouds above Mount Taylor. The car climbs a steep hill lined with pines before descending into a shallow valley speckled with yellow and brown boulders. My uncle leans back in the driver's seat. "There it is. Marquez."

Directly ahead, across a jagged arroyo, stands a few dozen houses scattered like wooden blocks across a landscape as rough as rattlesnake hide. Many of the homes have crumbled into the brush, but I can see the white propane tanks and black utility lines of the few remaining inhabitants.

My mother touches my shoulder. "We made it."

While my uncle shifts into low gear to approach the arroyo, I look around the valley to see if I recognize any landmarks, but I don't. "Where's the cave?"

My uncle points to an outcrop of pink boulders to my right. "By that formation."

I roll down my window for a clearer view. Between the pines I see a wall of sandstone sloping down the hill like the folds of a cloak. Below it, the black mouth of a cave. At that moment I remember— sliding down the smooth rock pretending to be a conquistador searching for gold. My grandfather, Carlos, stands at the cave opening, fedora tipped back, speaking in Spanish to my mother, who stares into the hollow at the blue-robed woman inside. "Is that really it?"

My uncle frowns. "One way to find out."

He switches off the ignition and steps outside while my mother snatches up her sunhat to follow. I hike ahead of them both, anxious to find the cave, and cut across a small ravine just south of the car before disappearing into the thick stands of pine. In the distance, I hear their voices.

"Look at this. A fossil!"

"And here. Another one."

Grinning at the echoes of my childhood, I search the ground myself, marveling at how every stone and root seems more vibrant under the noonday sun, as if I have awakened from a daydream, or rather, as if I have touched ground I was not sure existed. A particularly vivid stone catches my eye—ochre with a scarlet deposit twisting like an artery through the center. Turning its oval shape in my fingers, I almost see a living thing with its own past and story, like the artifacts in my mother's home. I begin to imagine: Maybe it was formed with actual blood, from the throat of a jackrabbit under an eagle's claw, or maybe during the birth of an ancient child, preserved in sandstone.

Next, I pause before a cholla grown into a cross, or crucifix, as a living testament of endurance. Then I see umbilical roots stretching from one sage bush to another, then angel-wing leaves, then my grandfather's creased face in the sand—everywhere affirmations, like my mother's horseshoe, that I, too, was meant to come. Light with adrenaline, I gather my discoveries into a pile.

My mother's voice rises through the trees. "Where are you? You've got to see this."

I slip the bloodstone in my pocket and follow the echo to a sandy wash where I find her and my uncle, hands on their hips, gazing down at their own collections of weathered stones and knotted roots. "Where have you been?" my mother asks. "You've missed everything."

I tell them about the crucifix cactus and the feathery leaves. Faces bright, they reveal their own discoveries: a white pottery sherd, a hawk feather, and a chunk of cedar as creased as a medicine man's face. Chattering like a couple of squirrels, they carry their artifacts to the car.

Instead of following them, I leave my pile behind and hike toward the slope above the cave. Cresting the hill, I find my path blocked by a barbed wire fence.

"Oh, no," my mother says, joining me. "It wasn't here last time."

I grab the wire, strung as tight as guitar strings.

My uncle stands beside us, arms folded, then walks the length of the chest-high barrier, testing the tension with both hands, jiggling the wooden posts, searching for weak spots.

Watching him, I notice the breeze has stilled and the sparrows have fallen silent, the entire hillside is holding its breath. I feel exposed suddenly, as if we're doing something wrong, trespassing, and someone was watching our every move. "I don't think we should cross."

My uncle steps on the bottom strand. "Why not?"

"Because someone put this fence here for a reason."

My mother rubs her hands. "Maybe he's right. I don't think I can fit under there."

Shaking his head, my uncle pulls up the middle strand with one hand and pushes down the bottom strand with his shoe, creating a narrow space for us to crouch through. "I'll hold it for you."

My mother looks at me, hands me her hat, and lowers herself under.

I survey the hills again, then duck under as well.

My uncle slips through a moment later. Wipes his hands on his jeans. "Let's look inside."

We sidestep down a hillside of loose gravel and prickly pear. Halfway to the bottom, my mother tugs my shirt. "Look at this. Bits of china." She bends to one knee and pinches a shard of porcelain from the sand. "See the cobalt paint. It's probably imported from Spain. And look. Another one. This must have been the original village site." My uncle joins her and rakes the sand with his fingers as if searching for loose change. "You're right. There are pieces everywhere."

I touch the stone in my pocket, acutely aware of our isolation, and feel again the stillness of the valley, but the pull of the cave is even stronger, so I walk ahead. A dozen yards from the entrance, I begin to see shapes inside—peeling whitewashed walls, the remnants of wooden shelves, what appears to be a blue fresco of the Virgin Mary—just as my grandfather and mother described.

I move toward the opening. A voice echoes from the village.

"What are you looking for?"

❧

We enter the village on foot. The road is covered with melon-sized rocks as it dips into the arroyo, impassible by car. Picking our way through the debris, we argue about crossing the fence.

"I have a right to be here," my mother says. "My family has ties to this land."

"We didn't do anything wrong," my uncle adds. "We should go back for your things."

I want to agree with them, I say, but don't know that I can. I'm still uneasy about the notion of trespassing, or altering a place we hope to preserve. Growing up, that thought never occurred to me, although we crossed our share of property lines, because we weren't pothunters. We didn't loot or steal. We didn't sell what we found. The artifacts we collected were rusted, broken, abandoned, or thrown away. That's why we wanted them—because they were forgotten. When we wriggled under a fence, it wasn't so much a transgression as it was a return to ground our relatives once walked. But now that I live so far away, I'm not sure what to think. "Maybe they don't want visitors," I say.

My mother frowns. "Maybe."

We work through the arroyo and up the other side passed a crumbling stone house where I thought I heard the voice. Skirting the edge of the back wall, I stumble over the severed head of a cow —its eye sockets hollow and its black hide peeling from its sun-bleached skull—and I think immediately of the pit bull carcass in Cubero graveyard. My mother covers her mouth.

On the other side of the house, three men size us up from across a weedy field. One wears a red T-shirt, another a blue button-up shirt, and the third a yellow Lakers jersey. Their faces are shadowed beneath their baseball caps. They stand before a shallow trench, shovels in hand.

The blue shirt says something to the red shirt. They laugh.

After a long silence, my mother cups her hands to her mouth and in a mix of English and Spanish shouts the story of her father's journey from Santa Fe to Marquez, rattling off family names and birthplaces, and introducing my uncle as a priest and me as her wayward son from Denver.

"I brought him here when he was little but he doesn't remember a thing," she says, throwing her hands in the air. "I'm almost eighty years old now and I want him to see this land once more before I die. My father always said he spent one of the most beautiful winters of his life in Marquez. The people here were very kind. They treated him like their own. And he never forgot."

The man in red tips back his cap. The others turn to him.

"How did you find us?" he yells.

My uncle shrugs. "My father showed us the way."

The man in red relaxes his shoulders and extends his hand. His grip is strong and his fingers callused. He's short and stocky, probably in his mid-thirties, but with his sunburned skin and crow's feet, appears ten years older. When he smiles, white teeth flash beneath a bushy black mustache.

"We wondered what brought you up here," he says. "I told my cousin, 'This is the first time I've seen anyone in a car.' Didn't think you could make it without a truck."

My uncle laughs. "We almost didn't."

The man turns out to be a descendant of Eliseo Marquez, whose family once owned practically every rock and juniper from Mesita del la Madera to the Santa Rosa peaks, but over the years, as ranching became harder and settlers moved east near the Rio Grande, the one-hundred-and-forty-year-old village gradually emptied. The man and his cousins live in Albuquerque, but stop by to check on things. They used to come once a month, but now less often. He used to bring his two daughters so they'd remember their roots, but they became frightened during sudden storms.

He leans on his shovel. "When the rain comes down, it really comes down. That arroyo you crossed can go from bone dry to a flash flood in seconds. Sounds like a stampede. You can barely hear yourself talk. And when the lightning hits one of those tin roofs, it's like a bomb."

About a year ago, the village bridge washed out. The state was supposed to fix it, but never did. In fact, just before we arrived, a few workers drove up in a dump truck loaded with lumber and steel, but when they saw the storm clouds, they turned tail and left.

"We worried about that, too," my uncle says, glancing behind him. "Getting caught."

The man frowns at the thunderhead to the west. "Might look that way, but it hasn't rained here all summer. Clouds gather around

Mount Taylor but pass us by. And we need the rain, too. We've never had such a dry year. It's strange, though. It just won't rain here."

He slips a hand under his cap. Scratches his head. "What was your father's name again?"

My mother repeats the story. The man folds his arms. He doesn't remember any Candelarias, but his grandfather did trade with farmers from Corrales, so maybe that was our family. My mother, eager for details, relays what her father had said about the cave—that it had been an open-air shelter with a potbelly stove, shelves built into the rock, tables, chairs, kerosene lamps, and a mural of the Virgin Mary, who gave her protection to the settlers crossing hostile Navajo and Apache territory.

The man smiles. His companions smile. "It's true. The cave was a sanctuary."

My mother places a hand on her chest. "I knew it. Your village is blessed."

The man wipes his forehead. "Not anymore. We've lost so much. And we lose more every day. Whenever we visit, something else is gone. Soon there won't be anything left."

Sweeping a hand over the horizon, he explains how the village land has been carved away by government officials seeking mineral rights, corporate ranchers seeking pasture, and hunters seeking hunting grounds. He and his family can't even walk a path they walked for generations—Las Palmas.

He points toward a low slumping hill just north of the village. When he was a boy, his grandfather carried him on his shoulders to a wellspring at the top—a pond of clear water surrounded by palm fronds. His family always considered the oasis a sign that settlers had chosen the right spot to live. Each Easter, families climbed toward the summit to give thanks.

"But if I go now," he says, squaring his shoulders, "I could be prosecuted for trespassing."

His companions grip their shovels. One spits.

And it's not just the government, the man in red continues. Thieves steal, vandals vandalize, and black marketeers scavenge the homes for religious art—taking even the church bell.

"A few years ago, someone hitched up one of my grandfather's wagons and hauled it off. Me and my cousin found it outside a new restaurant in Albuquerque with the landscaping. We told them it was ours, but they didn't care. 'Where's your proof,' they said. They don't offer payment. They don't say thanks. They just take it. People come in here and act like this place is theirs."

Touching the bloodstone in my pocket, I glance at my mother and uncle, who ignore me.

"They haven't taken everything," I say. "Not yet."

The three of them look at me for the first time.

"True," the red shirt says. "They haven't taken everything."

He gestures to a rectangular building of ochre stones. "That was a post office. My great-grandfather built it about a hundred years ago. The floors and windows are gone, but the roof's still there." Next, he points over my shoulder toward another stone building to the south. "That was the schoolhouse. It still has walls, windows, roof, everything. And with the wind we get out here? And the rain? It's a miracle they're standing. Go ahead and look."

We walk over and peek through the window. The floorboards have buckled, but the tongue-and-groove ceiling still holds. The walls have plaster. There's even a blackboard.

I picture young grandfather, Carlos, rail thin, standing before the class with his shy smile, demonstrating the cursive letters the nuns had taught him, adding flourish to his signature "C."

Opposite the blackboard on the south wall, I notice another marking so stark it startles me from my daydream—an "A," painted red, with a circle around it. Beside it, a black pentagram.

My uncle folds his arms. "Explains why they haven't had rain. The village is cursed."

The man in blue removes his sunglasses. He's a deacon in Albuquerque. He should have seen the markings, he tells us. He should have known. What should he do?

"Holy water," my uncle says. "Sprinkle the wall."

The man kicks a stone with his boot. "Can you do it, Father? Give us a blessing?"

My uncle asks us to join hands, closes his eyes, and prays—for the village, for its people, for the rain that won't come, for the difficult tasks before each of us. My mother looks at me. "Amen."

The man in red checks his watch and glances back at the trench he and his cousins had begun to dig. We shake hands and say goodbye. The three men drag their shovels up the road.

A mile from Marquez, before returning to Albuquerque, my uncle rubs his eyes, parks the car, and asks my mother for a snack. She reaches into the ice chest for cherries, apples, tortillas, and hard cheese. We watch the sky while we eat. The rainclouds, just as the men said, skirt the village.

"Sad," my mother says to no one in particular. "The New Mexico I knew is gone. All gone."

I spit a cherry pit into my palm. "What about those men?"

"Pobrecitos. I wish I could help them."

"But you did. The blessing."

My uncle turns to me. "We should go back for your rocks."

"After what they said? About tourists?"

"We are *not* tourists." My mother flips off her hat. "We know the history. My family has ties here. I'm saving artifacts—rescuing them—so my grandchildren will know."

"Still, it doesn't seem right."

"Why not? They're beautiful. Let's go get them. For your children in Denver."

"No." My uncle steps outside to stretch his legs. "If he doesn't want them, let them be."

Nodding, my mother turns to the hill where the man and his grandfather found the wellspring of palms. Her face warms. And I begin to understand: She brings me to these places to bear witness, to see the land as it exists now, to see that impermanence is the point. The past clarifies the present. To her, artifacts represent balance, even grace. In her pockets, markers of faith.

The car door swings open. My uncle opens his hand. "Guess what I found?"

My mother gasps. "A horseshoe. Just like the other one."

"I didn't even have to look for it," he says. "I opened the car door and there it was. Right in front of me. Sticking up through the dirt in the middle of the road."

I lean forward for a better look. "Quite a coincidence."

He fires the ignition. "There are no coincidences."

⁊

Wind blasts the car onto the shoulder of Interstate 40. The sky crackles with lightning.

"Hold on," my uncle says. "We can outrun it."

The speedometer hits 80, 85, 90...

My mother tightens her seatbelt. I slip the bloodstone from my pocket and roll it in my palm. Sand flakes onto my skin—pale yellow, as fine as pollen. With two fingers, I rub it in.

My uncle eases off the gas as we roll up Nine Mile Hill just west of Albuquerque. Glancing in the rearview mirror, he laughs. "Look at that. Just in time."

Behind us on the horizon, Marquez, blue with rain.

Two Halves

ONCE MORE into the desert, this time to Seboyeta, a two-hundred-and-sixty-year-old Spanish land grant village a few hours west of Albuquerque, not far from Marquez. My mother wants me to see a shrine dedicated to Saint Bernadette, patroness of shepherds as well as the poor, sick, and persecuted. She wants me to see another testament of faith and perseverance. She wants me to believe.

"We live in a world of miracles," she says, gazing out the car window. "They're everywhere. All around us. They call to us through nature. You go to a place you've never visited and know you've been there before. Or you answer a question before it's been asked. We all feel it. We all sense it. But we don't always pay attention. It's as though we have a veil covering our eyes. Yet, you can see through it if you try—if you're willing. And if you don't. . . What a heart breaking way to live."

Her words linger like the dust in the afternoon light—clear for a moment, drifting away. In the silence, we stare straight down the road, a narrow belt of sand and grass between an alfalfa field on the east and a granite wall to the west so charred by the sun it resembles a side of burned beef. Hot air blasts me in the face. I breathe in the aroma of history: dried weeds, old wood, and stone.

Seboyeta once stood in Navajo territory, a target of constant attacks despite a ten-foot wall and a contingent of soldiers. When only fifteen village men remained, survivors marched a thousand miles to the government in Chihuahua and begged for return to Spain. The Viceroy ordered them to honor their colonization contract. Villagers did as they were told, but built a shrine in a secluded cave where they hid during raids. And they promised: If Saint Bernadette would protect them, they would tend to her memorial as long as the village stood. They installed pews. An altar. Endured.

When my mother tells the story, I see it so clearly—Los Portales, The Gateway, a cave aglow in candlelight, the people of Seboyeta huddling before a wooden saint as their prayers rise with the smoke and incense, drawing strength from the stone sanctuary, from the land.

The car fishtails in the thick sand. Stones thud against the oil pan. Approaching the road's end, my mother sits up straight, and points to a cluster of willows below the cliffs.

"There. Beyond the trees. I can't wait for you to see it."

Before I can slow to a full stop, she scoops up her sunhat, pushes the door open, and hurries ahead, disappearing around a bend. I lock the car and trot after her, but pause at the echo of water—a stream or a river as loud as wind through mountain pines, murmuring like ambient voices. When I catch up to her in a meadow and describe the sound, she nods.

"Yes. I hear it, too. Strange, isn't it?"

Removing her sunglasses, she points above the grassy clearing toward a natural amphitheater a few hundred feet west of us—a one-story hollow scooped from solid rock.

"The shrine."

I squint in the noonday sun. The formation startles me—pale yellow, almost wooden, as though carved from a santero's blade, with creases and folds like the robes of Saint Bernadette herself. Swallows dart in and out of the opening and a creek trickles down from the base of the shrine toward an oasis of ferns, shrubs, reeds, and wild flowers. At the back of the cave wall, I can make out splashes of color—the pale blue of a Virgin Mary statuette, the whitewash of a concrete altar, the red of plastic carnations, the pink of votive candles. And I hear it again, the murmuring, echoing not from the creek, but somewhere I can't pinpoint, the trees or the rocks, all around.

My mother makes the sign of the cross.

Glancing into the creek bed before us, I notice a scattering of half-buried artifacts washed down from the altar—a sun-bleached deer bone, a faded plastic rose, a few white beads, and a water-stained handkerchief unfolding like wings. I lean forward for a closer look and something else catches my eye—two black-and-white pottery sherds shining in the mud like coins, two halves of a heart shape held in place by hair-thin roots, pieces of the same vessel, broken yet still connected.

My mother places a hand on my shoulder. "You were meant to find it."

The image is so striking, so unavoidably at my feet, I begin to think she's right.

Bending to one knee, she gathers a few daisies and heads up the footpath toward the altar.

I pick up one half of the sherd, but leave the other embedded in the sand.

With this offering, I follow.

Five

imprint [*n.* im-print; *v.* im-print]

ORIGIN: late Middle English (originally as emprint); from Old French *empreinter,* based on Latin imprimere, from in- *'into'* + *premere* 'to press.'

noun

1. a mark made by pressure

2. a core concept describing how the past affects the present

Animal Behavior, Psychology

1. rapid learning that occurs during a brief receptive period, typically soon after birth, and establishes a long-lasting behavioral response to a specific individual or site.

2. (of a young animal) come to recognize (another animal, person, thing) as object of habitual trust

• a critical period when an animal develops a concept of identity

• a process whereby the focal entity comes to reflect elements of its environment during a sensitive period; and the persistence of imprints despite subsequent environmental changes.

Once imprint learning is 'fixed' it is not likely to be forgotten or unlearned

verb

1. to plant firmly on the mind, or memory

In His Pockets

Dreams of. . . Carlos

He is born a Candelaria, after Our Lady of the Light, in the village of Puerto de Luna, the door of the moon. His father dies when he is nine and his mother marries a man who refuses to raise another's son. Carlos is shipped off to a Santa Fe boarding school, but runs away whenever he can. Sometimes he makes it home across a hundred miles of sand, but his tearful mother sends him away before her husband returns. Carlos lingers by the road, watching his family eat supper.

. . . Desolina

Abenicio prays for a son. When a second daughter arrives instead,
he dresses her in denim, bobs her thick auburn hair, and carries her
to the corral while he works the horses. She grows to love it all—
black coffee and cigarette smoke, rope burns and wrestling, sit-
ting on her father's knee during a game of poker, reading hands
of diamonds and spades. One morning, she fills one of Abenicio's
empty wine bottle with sheep's blood and sets it beside the road for
the borracho of a mailman. From the bushes, she watches while
he drinks deep, drops to his knees, and heaves up a darkness from
somewhere deep within, staining the pale blond sand.

. . . Carlos

He dreams of a cave with walls painted white and a woman in robes of blue. He knows in his heart it is a memory of Marquez, and still he aches for that place—warm ground to rest, embraced by the land, with a kind woman's eyes upon him.

. . . Desolina

In sleep, she wanders the Corrales camposanto, seeking buried jars
of gold coins. Among the black widows, she digs vessels of light,
and awakens convinced it is there—treasure, she says, at the tips
of her fingers, within the nests of bone.

. . . Carlos

He rides boxcars to Denver and beyond and stands alone in rivers of faces. He works with his hands and he works with his heart and he makes himself anew—Charlie Boy, polished shoes, tailored suit, change in his pockets.

. . . Desolina

She watches him from across the sala sipping apricot brandy and smiling with shy eyes. He has come for her sister but will leave with her, warmed by her prairie-fire passion. Charlie Boy, she says to herself, then says aloud. He has seen the ocean.

Within the Fiber

Dreams of. . . Migration

Carlos drives at midnight, when the desert cools beneath a granite moon, from Corrales to Los Angeles, and back again, fighting the headwinds toward a better life. Desolina sleeps in the passenger seat and the five kids sprawl in back. My mother watches him while he drives—wide-awake with his bulto face, knuckles white on the wheel, tires humming beneath them, mile after restless mile. Turning away, she stares into the black-velvet night, a spinning compass, unsure whether she is coming or going. Shadow-men wave from the roadside. Tall and lanky. Ten-gallon hats. Cactus-needle skin. Arizona. Their drive has only begun.

. . . Mementos

Carlos punches a clock in the San Pedro shipyards painting de-
stroyers so tall they touch the sky. He works fourteen-hour shifts,
six days a week, following a steam whistle's wail. My mother waits
curbside each night for his peeled-almond smile to brighten her
day. A whiff of turpentine. A peck on the cheek. Into her palm he
presses a surprise—a stick of Double Mint, a cat's eye marble, a
Cracker Jack toy, a shiny, new dime. Always, he remembers.

. . . the Blackout

Each night, the city goes black, silent beneath a cloak. Military policemen move from house to house, rapping mail slots with their batons. Desolina sets candles on tables and shelves and hands my mother a match. Sirens wail. Searchlights rake the clouds. Between my mother's fingers, a trembling flame.

. . . Fiber

*During air raid drills, my mother's first-grade teacher sends the
class to a basement shelter with beddings brought from home. My
mother chooses a Navajo blanket striped red, white, black, and gray.
Desolina sews on a slipcover to keep the coarse wool from scratch-
ing her skin, but my mother pulls it off to breathe in the scent of
memory—piñon smoke, bacon grease, black coffee, rosewater.*

. . . What She Sees

Sacred Heart Elementary holds an art contest. Draw something happy, the teacher tells her second-grade class. From butcher-block paper comes lipstick tulips, sunflower suns, stick-figure mommies, lollipop balloons. My mother sketches the llano—sky turquoise-pink, clouds lavender-green, rocks purplish black, sand rawhide brown. "Where did you learn to draw like that?" her teacher asks. My mother can't explain. It's what she sees when she closes her eyes.

. . . How They Are Seen

Another move—from Long Beach to Compton, from apartments to bungalows. At the south end of the block stands a market owned by a Jewish couple. Beside it an Italian butcher. Across the intersection a Mexican shoe store and barbershop. To the east of my mother's three-room flat, an Anglo family named Brown. To the west, an Anglo family named Lewis. The Browns keep to themselves, while the Lewises release their sons and daughters into the street to play. My mother's family gets along with everyone, and fits in everywhere—their ethnicities ambiguous. Carlos has blue-black hair and olive skin. Desolina is a freckled redhead. My mother's older brother has towhead curls, and her sisters mahogany waves. Until she is ten, my mother has a milky complexion and ash blonde hair. The Jewish grocer grins at Desolina. The Italian butcher pats Carlos on the back. The Mexican cobbler nods at them with respect. Even so, my mother can tell, there are questions behind the smiles, and a word to describe her family: Different.

. . . Oz

One summer, my mother's uncle, Gilo, visits from Corrales. He is
the youngest of Desolina's brothers, and spoiled rotten because
of his fair skin, blond hair, and pale green eyes—the image of
Abenicio. Gilo has never been to Los Angeles, so my mother takes
him to the corner market for ice cream. They stroll along the side-
walk, hand in hand, turning heads as they go, she in her school-
girl plaids and he in his pearl-button Western shirt, Dorothy and
the Scarecrow in the Land of Oz. Halfway to the intersection, a
gang of pachucos block their path.

"Orale," the biggest one says. "Where are you going, gringo?"

The pachucos circle them.

"Long way from Texas, no?"

The big one flicks off Gilo's hat.

"Who do you think you are? The Lone Ranger? Hi, ho
Silver!"

My mother turns to run.

In Spanish, Gilo says his name is Perea. He's visiting from
New Mexico.

The pachucos fall over themselves, laughing. They punch
Gilo's arm, pinch his pale cheek, and carry him on their shoulders, one of their own.

. . . Coco

He leans against the barbershop wall with a thumb in his sus-
penders and a matchstick between his teeth, chin high and half-
smiling, as if he owns everything in sight. And in this Southland
neighborhood, he does.

They call him Coco. Coconut. Dark brown skin and rock-hard
shell, short and stocky, with pockmarked cheeks, curly black hair,
and eyes as sharp as an Aztec blade. From the corner, he watches
everything and everyone, reading passerbys like the odds of the
daily double—what fathers do for a living, what time mothers
visit the market, which children belong to whom.

"Buenas tardes," he says, flashing a gold-tooth smile "Lovely
day."

He is like nothing my young mother has seen—so unlike the
teenage boys in New Mexico, with their blue jeans and Western
shirts. Coco favors double-pleated tama trousers, starched white
button-up shirts, shoulder-padded carlango jackets, and on the
weekends, wide-brimmed tando hats with single tapa feathers. A
gold watch chain dangles to his knees as he struts down the street
alongside other pachucos, as proud as roosters, owning their bar-
rios, unafraid of the Anglos and the storm-cloud threats of the
Zoot Suit Riots.

What fascinates my mother most, though, are his shoes. Instead of the patent-leather, pointed-toed, French-style "callos,"

Coco prefers Mexican huarachas. But not the ordinary leather-thonged Mexican-Indian sandals. His huarachas are dyed oxblood, polished to a reflective gloss, and fitted with a platform of nine custom soles—modified, glamorized, and urbanized, not unlike Coco himself. When he catches my mother peeking at them, he lifts his foot. "Que suave, no?"

He likes my mother and her humble family. Whenever they pass, he offers her a choice from his five-flavor roll of Life Savers. Always, she declines. She doesn't like his crooked smile, acne scars, dark wet eyes, and the way he seems to know something about her she doesn't. Only when her father nudges her does she accept the candy—cherry, sweet as a votive candle. Coco laughs under his breath.

No one defies him. No one tries. Once, the butcher stood tall at the corner, thick arms folded, and told the pachucos to clear out.

Coco spat at his feet. Sauntered away.

The following Sunday, when the butcher shop closed, Coco and his boys strolled up the street collecting garbage cans filled with a week's worth of refuse: eggshells, soup cans, coffee grounds, moldy bread. One by one, they surrounded the butcher's baby blue Ford Coupe, then Coco, as calm as though he were rinsing the car with soapy water, emptied the trash onto the windshield. Hooting and hollering, the others joined in. Coco swung a baseball bat at the chrome grill. "Home run!"

My mother sees Coco one last time leaning against the butcher shop wall, soaking in the afternoon sun while she carries a shopping list to the market. She glances at him, turns away, glances back. He grins. Reaching into his pocket for the candy, someone, or something, catches his eye, perhaps the shimmer of a rolling silver dollar, and he pushes away from the wall to chase it. At the edge of my mother's vision, a shadow—a black Buick sedan running the four-way stop sign.

A thud. A big ragdoll—a man in pleated khaki—tumbling into the air.

My mother freezes. A shape sails toward her through the cloudless sky, a sparrow or a crow, she thinks, and lands at her feet. She stares at the shape several minutes, not understanding, until the nine platform soles snap into focus.

Shop doors open. Women scream. An old man emerges from the Buick, hands trembling. "He came out of nowhere. . ."

My mother lifts the sandal from the gutter, and for a moment, in the glossy red-brown leather, she sees it—a flash of light.

. . . Secret Spaces

The house in Victorville arrives by flatbed diesel, rolling through the Apple Valley like a clipper ship on wheels. A crane lifts the white, wooden A-frame onto a foundation laid by Carlos, each pillar a promise to his family, to himself, to make it last. My mother explores every inch of the new home. Bay windows. Screened porch. Earthen basement. Airless attic. She brushes her hands along the seams for secret spaces. In them, she places dimes, crayons, buttons, artifacts.

. . . Reaching

*Carlos raises rabbits for a businessman cousin who owns a Holly-
wood restaurant serving French cuisine. The French like rabbit.
Cages crowd the yard. Each morning, my mother brings fresh water
and green pellets, but Carlos warns her—"They're not pets. Don't
give them names. Don't touch them." My mother visits anyway,
and reaches through the wire bars to stroke the silken faces.*

. . . Paper Dolls

*They pause before the camera on the lawn of a white Victorian
—ruffled dresses, satin bows, a pair of spring carnations. My
mother stands beside her younger sister, Ernestina, who kneels,
resting her fever-scarred heart. Three years apart, they are as
close as sisters can be, sharing socks, Raggedy Anns, pillows, and
prayers, my mother the watchful protector. In the portrait, they
stand unsmiling, my mother's gaze forward, and Ernestina's outside the frame, on the horizon.*

*She chokes on California smog and collapses after crossing a room.
Carlos drives the family back to Albuquerque, so Ernestina can
breathe free under the desert sky. For a time she does. Then one
morning, changing guest-room bedding in the bungalow of their
Aunt Molly, Ernestina points behind my mother to a radiance near
the window—a woman with open arms. Ernestina is certain. "An
angel."*

*They sit on the floor making paper dolls, knowing without know-
ing what comes on the wind—a thunderstorm of hot, humid air,*

and a night when Ernestina's heart finally flutters away. Ernestina will die in their father's arms, and my mother will bathe her with a cotton cloth, and dress her in a First Communion gown, and light the velorio candles. But on this morning in July 1944, there is none of that. There is only white sheets of paper, and little girls holding hands.

. . . a Swing

Wherever they live—California, New Mexico, California again
—Carlos makes my mother a swing. He loops a rope over a branch
and attaches a truck tire or a seat made from orange crates. My
mother rides for hours, legs pumping, rising.

. . . Second Skin

Molly is so different than anyone in my mother's family. So gen-
erous with her hugs and kisses. So glamorous with her Rita Hay-
worth curls, fashion-model legs, and high-heeled shoes. So sunny
in her pink silk dress with white rosebuds. And yet, in her heart,
she worries about having children. More than anything she wants
children, but at thirty-two, no matter how hard she prays, she can't.
When Desolina becomes pregnant with her sixth child, Molly, her
younger sister by two years, asks if she and her husband, Pete,
might adopt the baby to ease the burden—a request not unusual
back then among large farming families. Desolina agrees, but
once the baby is born and she sees the jet-black hair and china-
doll skin of her newest daughter, she points to my mother in the
delivery room corner.

"Take her instead," she tells Molly. And Molly does.

They live near downtown Albuquerque in a yellow bungalow by
the Santa Fe Railroad shops, where Pete works as a machinist. He
and Molly treat my mother like a princess. Saturday matinees at
the KiMo. Strawberry milkshakes at Walgreens. Living room par-
ties jitterbugging to the Andrew Sisters. My mother misses her

parents, loves her parents, but loves Molly, too. For the first time, my mother has her own room, and her own bed. Outside her window, morning glories.

A letter arrives at the ranch house from Pedro, the seventh of fourteen children. He's worried, he writes. He's been visited in his sleep by Molly, who came to him in his Army barracks in North Africa. She sat at the foot of his bunk and placed her hands on his cheeks. "Pray for me," she told him. "Estoy muerto."

May 22, 1945. A steam whistle in the rail yard. At the depot, men run to the tracks. Outside the yellow bungalow, sedans gather.

No one tells her. No one knows how. Ernestina had died the summer before, and maybe they think my nine-year-old mother can't handle the shock. Maybe they're too stunned with their own grief. My mother learns of her aunt's death only as she kneels before the open casket during the rosary, gazing down at the waxy cheeks dusted with rouge, the putty above the left eyebrow, the gap in the shirtsleeve between right elbow and right hand, and the painted lips trying to smile.

No one tells her about Molly hugging a cousin goodbye as he boarded a passenger train for a tour in the Pacific. No one tells her about Molly catching her heel as she leapt from the moving car onto the platform. No one tells her what the conductor says in the morning paper—"We were moving out of the station. I was closing the rear door of the second to the last car when this woman came up and said, 'Wait. I've got to get off!' When I told her, 'You can't get off now,' she pushed me aside and jumped. She fell or tripped. I don't know what happened."

No one tells my mother, but somehow she knows. And she remembers.

❧

Late night. The ranch house after the funeral. My mother is in the guest room trying to sleep when a voice drifts in from the kitchen —calling her name.

She pads down the hallway.

In a chair beside the kitchen stove, she sees a woman in a pale dress.

She rushes forward.

"Stop!"

Adelida grabs her shoulders from behind.

"But it's Molly," my mother says. "She's here. . ."

"No. Listen to me. She's gone."

Adelida faces the chair and makes the sign of the cross. "Leave this place. Go where you need to go but let this child be. God bless you. Rest in peace."

Adelida ushers my mother back to bed.

My mother remains awake, listening, but she never hears Molly again.

❧

A gift from Adelida—a pair of pajamas, pink with white rosebuds.

My mother wears them like a second skin.

At last, she sleeps.

. . . Independence

While Carlos punches a clock and Desolina visits friends, my mother cooks, cleans, shops, and watches her five younger siblings. She makes sure the light bill and grocery bill are paid on time. She registers herself for school. She earns As. Sings in church choir. Makes decisions. Follows through. At fourteen, she lives by the rules of her grandfather's ranch—with purpose. And she begins to understand a word that will give her strength in years to come: Independence.

The Heights

Dreams of. . . American Beauties

Albuquerque again. Six children and two adults in a three bed-room, one bathroom, cinderblock rectangle in the post-World War II subdivision boom. They leave the furrows of the Rio Grande valley for the cul-de-sacs of the Sandia Foothills "heights." The house is new. The house is theirs. They never move again. Carlos paves roads while my mother attends high school and the family gathers around the TV. All around the yard, Desolina plants flow-ers, especially the American Beauty.

. . . Flickering

My mother walks at dusk among the foothill boulders to stare across the valley. On the opposite rim, she can see Corrales lights, gradually flickering away.

. . . Winter

Abenicio winters in Southern California, where his ranch-weary sons settle after the war. With his tobacco cough and dwindling land, he welcomes the San Bernardino sun. Late one December night, a Cadillac slows to the curb of the house in the heights, and spirits Desolina across the Mojave Desert. Abenicio dies from a virus in his lungs and is buried a thousand miles from home.

. . . Beads

In sleep, Desolina sees an olive wood rosary, and in the morning, awakens to an aching sense of loss. She looks everywhere, but cannot find the beaded strand, and when they finally appear, she weeps. It is during a funeral, in a casket, in the hands of her mother, Adelida.

. . . the Weight

*Midnight. My mother's three youngest sisters sit awake in the
back room, giggling. From down the hallway, they hear the shuf-
fling of boots—step after rasping step. The girls, expecting Carlos
or Desolina, cover their heads with the bed sheet. Footfalls come.
From the hall. Into the room. Around the bed. The children hold
their breath. Beside them, a sigh, then a bed-spring squeak, then
a heavy weight on the mattress. Flipping back the covers, one of
them screams. Nothing there.*

. . . the Edge

Carlos snaps a black-and-white photo of my mother on a broad, flat boulder in the Sandia Foothills, where they often come to enjoy the silence. She sits on the edge wearing a dark, button-up blouse and a pale, pleated skirt, seventeen going on eighteen, squinting into the distance, beyond the frame, at something only she can see.

. . . Grace

In looks, she is Natalie Wood. In temperament, Grace Kelly. So mature, everyone says. So regal. So serene. On the Technicolor screen of the KiMo or El Capitan, my mother watches her other selves—The Searchers, To Catch a Thief.

. . . Want Ad

A classified ad in the afternoon paper—"Wanted: Bookkeeper. Fletcher Drugs." She recognizes the name—the pharmacy one block from her studio apartment just off Route 66 near the Public Library, where she spends afternoons lost in story. A silver bell tinkles when she opens the door, and from the soda fountain counter, a man looks up from his coffee. White smock. Salt-and-pepper hair. Watching her with Perry Mason eyes. My mother smiles. He snuffs his cigarette. Says hello.

. . . an Oasis

He is thirty years her senior, as old as Carlos himself, divorced, childless, recently widowed, and the last in his Midwestern family line. He is a heavy smoker with a failing heart who served in a Presidio hospital during World War II treating wounded soldiers shipped stateside from the South Pacific. At night, he sits alone in his North Valley home, a Civil Air Patrol captain, spinning the dials of a HAM radio set, listening for the celestial echo of voices.

He makes her laugh. She makes him smile.

He brings her to his Pueblo-style house on the edge of the Rio Grande farmland and buys her a Starlight silver Cadillac sedan with white walls, white leather interior, power steering, and muscular 365 engine. He hires her younger sisters at his pharmacy, and gives her an allowance for salons, luncheons, boutiques, herself.

In the evenings, they stand shoulder to shoulder mincing garlic, melting butter, and sipping chardonnay for gourmet dinners. They host parties. Plant roses.

Everyone agrees—their home is an island, an oasis.

. . . Keys

He surprises her. While shopping at a neighborhood market, they
notice a poor man and his children who live behind their Pueblo-
style house in a clapboard shack. The man is a ghost of overalls and
a fedora, and his daughter and son, no more than seven or eight,
wear patch-quilt jeans and white T-shirts gone gray. They stand
with wrinkled sacks picking through potatoes and onions to carry
back home. My father sets aside his grocery cart and walks over
to talk. The man looks down and eventually nods. My father hands
him the keys to his luxury Plymouth sedan.

The man needed his help, he tells my mother, later.
So he helped.

. . . the Fall

He falls from the stepladder of some household chore, a curtain drawn over his eyes. Loose change spills from his pockets and rolls across the waxed hardwood planks into the dark grate of the living room floor furnace, rattling on its way down.

Six

shrine |SHrīn|

ORIGIN: Old English *scrīn* 'cabinet, chest,' of Germanic origin; related to Dutch *schrijn* and German *Schrein*, from Latin *scrinium* 'chest for books.'

noun

a place regarded as holy because of its associations with a divinity or a sacred person or relic

- a place containing memorabilia of a revered person or thing
- a casket containing sacred relics
- a reliquary
- a niche or enclosure containing a statue or other object

verb [with obj.] literary

enshrine: preserve in a form that ensures it will be protected

Ascent

"*Grace fills empty spaces, but it can only enter where there is a void to receive it, and it is grace itself which makes this void.*"

—Simone Weil, *Gravity and Grace*

THE PEACOCK came in the rain, carried to our doorstep by boys who found it raiding campground trash in the Jemez Mountains. Legs tangled in black twine, throat clogged with fishing line, it burrowed its head in my mother's shoulder. "Sol pavo," she whispered. "Sun bird." With tweezers and cotton cloth she tended the thread-bound tongue and with bath towels and bed sheets made a laundry room nest, then flicked off the light to watch it sleep. The next morning, it left her a feather, blue and green, shimmering like an eye.

The owl arrived on Beggar's Night, in my big brother's jacket, after he found a nest shot full of holes on the ditch bank. Our mother named the hatchling Tirzah, after a beautiful city in the bible, and released her into our home to fly.

On summer days while we swam the streams of the Jemez Mountains, the owl slept in the shade, tethered to a piñon branch with turquoise yarn. One afternoon we waded too long, slept in the sun, and woke to an empty branch and a broken string. We searched for hours but found nothing. Turning to leave, my mother saw a pair of yellow eyes shining from a streamside shrub, bright as dimes. "Tirzah," she whispered, and extended her finger. Wind gusted. Sparrows flew free. The owl hopped on, held tight.

The parrots escaped, and escaped again, slipping through wire bars and lifting latches with crescent beaks to unravel Navajo rugs and nibble the edges of *Time*. Maybe it's wrong, my mother thought, to buy a pair of dime store lovebirds as bright green as the jungles from which they came, to name them Allegria and Mariposa, and then restrain them. Then, one morning, while filling their bowls with seeds and fresh water, she found a nest of yarn and magazine shavings. Inside it: an egg, perfect as a pearl.

As these words were said, the birds began to open their beaks, stretch their necks, spread their wings and bow to the ground, endeavoring by motion and song to manifest their joy. Saint Frances rejoiced with them, charmed by their beautiful voices. He made the sign of the cross and gave them leave to fly. The birds rose into the air following the cross he had made—one flew east, another west, one to the south, and one to the north, carrying on their tongues all they had heard.

—From "The Little Flowers of St. Francis of Assisi"

He came to my mother in dreams. Stood at our front step and knocked. She was glad to see him, my father, standing there with his silver hair, sad eyes, immaculate white smock. Always, she let him in.

My second grade teacher, herself a widow, brought my family a crippled snow goose. It limped into our backyard with its loose hip and blind eye and fell beside the wishing well. With a cotton cloth and garden hose my mother cleaned yellow stains from white feathers and whispered the name she had chosen—Washoti, after the gentle Indians of the Great Lakes. "Pet him," she told me. "Talk to him." Reaching out, I stroked his crooked wing.

Alone in the mornings she walked barefoot through the backyard grass gathering feathers. She wrapped them in wax paper and placed them inside her nickel-plated hope chest, beside a wooden tobacco urn, a two-sided silver mirror, and a crown of Penitente thorns.

She sketched outside to clear her mind, practicing techniques she learned in art class—tone, texture, volume, depth. Sometimes she invited me to join her and we sat side by side transforming found objects into still lifes. Try as I might, I could not make my eggshell rise from the page.

Holding my pencil still in her hand, she squinted at the broken sphere. "See. Right there. Within the shadow, reflected light."

Cobwebs grew thick between the bare studs of my mother's unfinished studio. Shoulder strained from tending trumpet vines, she could not raise a broom high enough to sweep them away. Gauzy ribbons drifted like ghosts. One morning she woke to a flicker between rafters, a hummingbird, tangled in sticky threads. Dragging a chair to the light, she scanned the beams for the teardrop body of a black widow spider. Seeing none, she reached through the web as if passing fingers through flame. Tiny wings buzzed. The tweezer beak opened without a sound. With a washcloth she wiped clean bound feathers of blue and green and soothed with a whisper the hatchling held to her heart. She stepped from the chair toward the wishing well in the grass, and gazing up, she opened her hands.

Portraits

"Don't grieve. Anything you lose comes round in another form."
—Rumi

SHE KNELT as a girl on the ranch house floor with sheets of butcher paper spread wide as the sky. With charred piñon kindling she dreamed through her fingers, rendering images so fine they might have been smoke. Day became night —an oil-lamp flame—and she wiped clean the page to begin again.

Her first portrait, her Tia Rita, orphaned as a girl, first a beggar then a maid, before marrying a drunk with fists of stone. On her palate my mother mixed turquoise, sunflower, cobalt, and sage, and remade her aunt in profile outside an adobe home, lugging a water bucket across the New Mexico sand, eyes down, back bent, stepping into the light.

Vaqueros. Canvas after canvas of roping scenes, branding scenes, herding scenes, riding scenes. Never dramatic, never romanticized, she painted solitary moments, stringing wire, or heading home, each man cut from the llano, rawboned, sunburned, faces of cedar, faces of clay.

๛

Landscape blankets of sand and scrub. Red arroyo. Black cottonwood crack. Clouds of feather and clouds of flame. Everywhere watering holes, shining from the sand, bright as mirrors, bright as change.

๛

Across from her church stood an art shop. On its door a silver bell. After my father died, my mother drifted down aisles of cadmium colors and empty frames. Between her fingers, charcoal ash.

๛

A quilt. Seventy-two black satin panels embroidered with pearl cotton thread. One memory per panel. Hand pump. Half moon. Screech owl. Spanish fan. Between the panels, flowers from her garden. Hollyhock. Honeysuckle. Fairy rose. Poppy. She called it, Memories.

๛

Her favorite artist was Salvador Dali, who said this: "One day, it will be officially admitted that what we have christened reality is an even greater illusion than the world of dreams."

With a long curved needle she pulled colored thread through manta. From her tapestry rose Los Hermanos Penitentes climbing a hill on Easter morning. Beneath a red sky they advanced in black silhouette. The first held a crucifix, the second a lantern, the third a heavy cross. The fourth raised a whip while the fifth read a bible and the sixth and seventh played flute and drum. None had faces but my mother knew them well. She had seen them in the eyes of her father.

Sheets of copper and sheets of brass, hammered into the hair combs and parlor fans she saw in her mind. At art show openings everyone said: from another place. Another time. Mesopotamia or Thebes. Her signature piece—a silver headband tapered to a widow's peak with a star opal in the center and purple braids at the temples, threaded with moonstones. She wore the crown only once. It fit her perfectly.

From ceramic, thumb-sized tribal masks of grief and joy and confusion and wonder, sewn to the edges of a labyrinth-pattern neckpiece. Between the masks, peacock feathers and guinea hen quills. In the folds, discs of copper and brass. She called it, Spirit Collar.

Her fine arts professor said: Make a box. A vessel. Explore exterior surfaces and interior spaces. She hammered a cube of fresh pine and lined the inside with iridescent folds of gold, emerald, crimson, and turquoise. In the center, she placed a purple ring pillow. On the pillow, she placed an ojime bead—Hanya, woman spirit, lost angel.

❧

I watched her under the white dining room light bringing dead cottonwood leaves to life with charcoal and conté. When I erased my paper to begin again, my mother leaned across the table to whisper her secret: Don't draw what you look at. Draw what you see.

❧

For the portrait of her grandmother, she spread a wide sheet of manta on the dining room table and sketched the old woman in profile, leaning back in a rocker, wearing a black dress of mourning, hands in her lap, head lowered in reflection. With yarn and a colcha needle, she rendered the topographic face, the iron gray hair, and the cottonwood hands. Within the tapestry folds, she stitched wedding bands, skeleton keys, rosary beads, and empty picture frames.

❧

For her self-portrait, she began with a four-panel window dug from an adobe ruin. In the upper left panel, she placed a black-and-white photo of her grandmother, wrinkled in smile, gazing toward the horizon. In the upper right panel, she placed a mirror streaked with sepia ink. In the lower left, she glued a blank postcard with a stamp from her birth year, 1935, and in the lower right, a bouquet of dried red roses. Draped over the entire frame, a veil of black Spanish lace. "Can you see it," she would ask me. "Can you see what I'm saying?"

For her final gallery installation, she selected a dozen arroyo stones from her unfinished wishing well. On the smooth gray surfaces she glued photo transfers of family she had lost. As a frame she chose the rusty rails of a broad iron bed. Within the frame, she laid the stones in an oval pile, as she had found them, sliding from the sand, revealed.

Artifacts

"*Every parting gives a foretaste of death, every reunion a hint of resurrection.*"

—Arthur Schopenhauer

MY MOTHER took a snapshot of our living room in the early sixties. Gray curtains. Gray vinyl easy chair. Gray davenport with square gray cushions. Silver ashtray. Polished hardwood floors. A safe, orderly reflection of her life in the seven years she knew my father. After he died, she rearranged our home completely. The walls were never bare again.

❧

She saw the stones in a roadside arroyo, round and flat, embedded like watermelon seeds in the pink Algodones sand. She filled our car trunk until the axle groaned and emptied her wheelbarrow onto the backyard grass. A wishing well, she said. She would make a wishing well. Her grandparents had a cistern on their ranch in Corrales. Each morning as a young girl, my mother lowered a bucket into the black depths. Rope slid through her fingers. Water dribbled down like pearls. When she called out, a voice answered.

❧

Bones. Dug from the badlands west of Albuquerque and pitched onto our roof to bleach blue-white in the summer sun. Cow skulls. Horse skulls. Ram skulls. Elk antlers. Wired to the front porch vigas and placed beneath the church bench, blooming from the shadows, bright as lilies.

❧

"Do you know what this is?" my mother would ask, guiding me by the hand through the rolling mesa above the Rio Grande. "It's an arrowhead. And this one is a bird point. You can tell by the chipped edges."

"Like this?"

"No. That's just a rock. Look closer. What do you see?"

❧

Each evening she wound an antique clock, a tabletop cathedral of walnut and glass, its face a harvest moon ghosted with pale blue numerals. She inserted a key beneath the seven and turned, whispering the count, until the spring strained, the gears clicked, and the pendulum swung on its horsehair tether.

On the hour, a silver bell.

❧

My mother found the rocker in a second-hand shop in Alameda, dusty and broken, as arthritic as her grandmother's knees. Back home on her porch, surrounded by C-clamps and glue, she reset the arms, legs, ribs, and seat, and placed the chair in the living room beside her reading lamp. Leaning back, she closed her eyes and smiled, raising her feet as though riding a swing.

On winter mornings, she sprinkled piñon incense over the living room floor furnace to conjure the warmth of the ranch house kitchen. Straddling the steel grate in her slippers, her flannel nightgown swelled with heat, and sparks swirled orange around her eyes, rising on the current.

As a girl, my mother watched her grandfather make nails in his blacksmith shop, clipping iron rods, filing down shiny tips, filling one coffee can after another, never sure he had enough. Later, as a grown woman, she harvested nails from abandoned barns and fallen fence posts and displayed them on her walls to accentuate the form—bent by burden, shaped by weight.

"Do you know what this is?" she would ask me.

"Barbed wire?"

"Yes. But what else?"

"A loop? From a fence post?"

"From a gate. You lift it to get inside. It's a key."

She placed the water bowl on the pottery case as the centerpiece of her artifact collection. Big as a melon and shaped from river clay, it balanced on the heads of Zuni women, and bore a painted roadrunner, symbol of swiftness, standing in a labyrinth of black and white. On the afternoon it fell, sherds like shrapnel, my mother, on hands and knees, recovered every piece, and under the white dining room light, filled the hairline cracks.

She scattered her mother's violet seeds beneath the pines where she hoped they would thrive in the half-sunlight, half-shade. The following spring, on the anniversary of her birth, the deceased woman appeared in my mother's dreams, arms raised, standing among the blossoms.

She drove with her father through the deserts of his youth. From the roadside sand they pulled a ladder, its pine rungs leading up and out. Together they lifted the broken frame into his pickup and leaned it against the eastern wall of our house, facing the sunrise.

Among her periwinkle and poppy, she found a hummingbird's nest on a fallen pine branch. Inside the nest, a dead hatchling, delicate as spun glass. With both hands, she placed the branch atop her pottery case, beside a rosary, a river stone, pocketknife, and a bowl of piñon ash.

"Look. A root. Beneath the chamisal bush."

"That dead thing?"

"It's not dead. Not at all. See the color? Bluish-black. Like a cottonwood at night. And the shape? Like grape vines or barbed wire."

"Or the veins of a heart."

"Exactly. Take it home. So you'll remember."

Returning home from the badlands after my father died, she stopped at Jemez Pueblo to rest. My mother met an old man who sat apart from the other village vendors with his work displayed before him on a blanket—rattles of squash and pumpkin shaped into the animals of his dreams.

"Beautiful," she told him. "So expressive."

He studied her face, all beauty and sorrow.

"Take one," he said. "As a gift."

She chose a teardrop gourd with moon eyes at one end and a fishhook tail at the other, painted with black and white and rust-red feathers.

The old man smiled.

"The flying serpent. Symbol of water, wind, rebirth."

Seven

nostalgia | nä'staljə, nə- |

ORIGIN: from Greek *nostos* 'return home' + *algos* 'pain.'

noun

'hypochondria of the heart,' which thrives on its symptoms.

Coined by ambitious Swiss student Johannes Hofer in his medical dissertation in 1688. Hofer attributed soldiers' mental and physical maladies to their longing to return home.

Considered in the 17th Century a curable disease akin to a common cold. Swiss doctors believed opium, leeches, and a journey to the Swiss Alps would cure symptoms. Doctors in the 18th and 19th centuries looked for a single cause—for a 'pathological bone'—yet failed to find the locus.

Nostalgia appears to be a longing for a place, but is actually a yearning for a different time—the slower rhythms of our dreams.

Odysseus longs for home.

Proust is in search of lost time.

For the wandering figure of Abraham home is always to come.

A rebellion against the modern idea of time: refusing to surrender to the irreversibility that plagues the human condition.

Shown to counteract loneliness, boredom, and anxiety. Makes people generous to strangers. Couples feel closer. On cold days, or in cold rooms, people use nostalgia to feel warmer.

A cinematic image of nostalgia is a double exposure or a superimposition of two images—home and abroad, past and present, dream and everyday life. The moment we try to force it into a single image, it breaks the frame, or burns the surface.

Nostalgia can be a poetic creation, a survival mechanism, a poison, a cure.

House of Sun

ON SUMMER nights when I was a boy, toads crept from the acequia behind our house to the streetlight at the front curb. Children
of the earth, Pueblo Indians called them, bringers of life and renewal.
I watched from my bedroom window as they pushed through mud
and gravel toward the swirl of mosquitos and the pulsing white
bulb, dying by the dozens, these gentle creatures, as headlights
rounded the curve and older boys arrived with firecrackers and
Little League bats. By the time I finished my prayers, a few made it
back. The next night, they began again.

Doctors could not help him. An eye exam found a tumor in my father's brain. The cancer had spread from his lungs to his lymph glands and although he could receive radiation treatments, at age fifty-eight, a heavy smoker with a failing heart, surgery was not an option. He entered the Veteran's Administration hospital for the final time in June 1964. Once a week my mother brought the five of us kids to visit, but ranging in age from six to sixteen months, we were too much for her to handle, too much for him, so we waited outside in the shady grass beside a parking lot. From a third floor window, our father parted the curtains, and waved.

Late afternoon. I snapped awake on the living room davenport—hot, tired, Beatle bangs plastered against my forehead. My mother was gone and my siblings were gone and my babysitter was nowhere in sight. Shadows crept in from the corners. Rubbing my eyes, I noticed the front curtains were closed. I didn't like the curtains closed, so I reached out and pulled, but they fell back in place, thick and gray and smelling of my father's ashtray. I tried again and they held firm, as if someone tugged from the other side. I began to cry. I couldn't find the opening. Couldn't let in the light.

My big brother would not cry. He kept asking our mother, "When is dad coming home?" The pediatrician recommended a child psychiatrist, who told her, "The boy is living in a fantasy world. Remove his father's things from the home. Show him his father is gone." My mother did as she was told and took away our father's things—his ashtray, his wristwatch, his ring, his sweater—and packed them in cardboard boxes. She placed them in the hallway closet and closed the door.

She baked in the afternoons. Peanut butter cookies. Oatmeal cookies. Cinnamon bread. Cherry pie. I would straggle into the kitchen after my nap to find her at the counter with a rolling pin and mixing bowl, gazing out the window. She and my father had been married seven years. In that time they had five children. Twenty-eight when he died, she never remarried. In the afternoon when my older siblings returned from St. Theresa elementary, we sat at the dining room table with napkins and milk while she balanced our baby sister on her knee, eyes alight with our chatter. She herself never ate a bite. The treats were ours alone, she said. She wanted only this—to see us smile.

I sat alone in the closet with his boxed-up things. Just sat there. Breathing in dust and mothballs. Door opened a crack to let in the living room light. Sometimes I brought the *National Geographic* with Buzz Aldrin on the cover, light as a ghost in zero gravity, impossibly far from home, moon headstone gray, sky bottomless black. From the slick pages I slipped a 45 record of real conversation between astronauts and Mission Control, then brushed my fingers along the plastic grooves.

We lived month to month on Veteran's Administration Survivor's Benefits and a Social Security pension that my father, who served in World War II, had paid into his entire working life but died before he could collect. No matter how well my mother planned—using all the resourcefulness and creativity she had learned on the ranch and in art school—the cupboards always seemed to empty before we crossed thirty days from the calendar. When the checks finally arrived on the first and third and we pushed our cart down the grocery aisle loading enough meat and milk and bread and fruit to carry us through another month, my mother allowed us a special indulgence—one Betty Crocker cake mix for each of us kids to bake while we watched our favorite TV shows, *Lost in Space* or *All In The Family*. Those cakes became the highlights of our weeks. Our months. They kept us going. They gave us something to look forward to, always ahead, just on the horizon.

She protested the Vietnam War. Talked three sisters through three divorces. Pinned "Nixon No" buttons to my fifth grade lapel. Switched *Jonny Quest* to the Watergate hearings. Studied fine art and Spanish in college. Illustrated books of Chicano poems and stories. And once, when Mountain Bell overcharged our phone bill and cut off our service, my mother visited First National Bank with a gallon-sized water bucket and asked the teller to fill it with enough pennies to match the amount of the $300 tab. At MA Bell she set the bucket on the accountant's desk. There, she said. Paid in full.

He called me Hercules. He watched me through the nursery window while I pushed myself up to frown at the squalling babies. He sat me in his lap while I gripped his index finger and pulled myself toward him, chin-up style, while he fed me Oreos and I gummed them whole. I would be a football player, he told my mother. Or a boxer. For me, my father had this hope—I would be strong.

Neighborhood boys stole tools from our yard. Beat up my brother. Whistled at my mother. Our vulnerability, she said, made them bold. Made them mean. One afternoon they stuck a cherry bomb in our mailbox and the blast rattled our windows. Instead of driving to Chase Hardware for a replacement she picked through a backyard lumber pile for a few planks of barn wood and with kitchen cabinet hinges and an antique handle crafted a weathered letterbox like the ones she grew up with on the ranch. On the door of the box she carved the silhouette of a Pueblo-style house with a tiered roof and front porch vigas like ours. Above the house she etched a Zia sun with parallel lines radiating from the four directions. Above the symbol she carved, Casa del Ninos del Sol.

"House of the Children of the Sun," she said, planting our new mailbox like a flag. "Like it?"

"House of sun." I said it out loud. Said it all day.

We visited her grandmother's ranch house, which looked to me like the hacienda in *The High Chaparral*. An old woman spoke to my mother in Spanish and watched me with smiling eyes. Spooked by the shadows, I headed outside to explore the yard, and lost myself in time. My mother found me an hour later beneath a mulberry bush, drunk on strange fruit, the sweetest I ever tasted.

On Halloween my family held a party. We invited all the cousins and aunts and uncles and made a night of it. We danced the limbo rock and played Pin the Eye on the Cyclops and offered root beer and Hershey bars for the best costume. The only rule: Nothing store bought. Only materials at hand.

I paired with my uncle, my mother's younger brother and art school partner, who had been raised on *The Outer Limits* and *The Twilight Zone* and introduced me to *The Lord of the Rings* and *The Seventh Voyage of Sinbad*. I told him that I wanted to be a Rivendell elf or a Persian sheik. That I wanted to wear robes or a cloak. That I wanted to be something magical and brave.

He scratched his wizard beard and nodded.

The party began at dusk. My brother arrived as a wolf man with wild hair and dirt smeared on his arms and face. My oldest sister came as a mummy wrapped in bed-sheet bandages. My middle sister dressed as a voodoo princess with a stuffed monkey on her shoulder and my little sister dressed as a sombrero-wearing bandito. My mother and uncle, ever ironic, came as themselves.

I wore two costumes in one—on the outside, a desert king in a bedspread cape, but on the inside, an elf with pointed ears made of masking tape.

My uncle called for quiet and brought me forward. All eyes turned to me as I peeled away the robes as if shedding layers of skin, revealing the boy within.

I won first prize.

One morning I woke to find the gray curtains gone. I stepped from the hallway into the living room to find my mother wiping the front window with paper towels and a turquoise bottle of liquid.

Everything clean. Everything white.

On summer nights before bed I rode my bike from one end of the block to the other, pushing though potholes and gravel toward a puddle of light beneath the curbside street lamp. Head down and thighs burning, I sailed through the blackest black until I approached the silvery glow of our house. Then I released the handlebars and sat upright—arms wide, flying.

Eight

home /hōm/

ORIGIN: Old English *ham* 'dwelling, estate, village,' from Proto-Germanic **haimaz* (cognates: Old Frisian *hem* 'village,' Old Norse *heimr* 'residence, world,' Danish *hjem*, Middle Dutch *heem*, Armenian *shen* 'inhabited,' Swedish *hem,* German *heim,* Gothic *haims,* 'village;' akin to haunt

noun
1. where something flourishes
   • INFORMAL where an object is kept
2. where a player is free from attack

verb [no obj.]
1. to focus upon intently
2. to move or be aimed toward with great accuracy
3. to return to by instinct after leaving
   • to fly back to after being released from a distant point

adverb
1. to or at:
   • the conclusion of something
   • the correct position

noun
1. where something is discovered:
   • the source

from PIE root **tkei*—to settle
   cognates:
   • Sanskrit *kseti,* 'abides'
   • Greek *keimai,* 'to rest'

Clearing

SHE APPROACHED our yard like a blank canvas, composing with lilacs, irises, sunflowers, cottonwood, and volcanic rock. Day by day our three-quarter acre rectangle of Albuquerque's North Valley grew into my mother's version of New Mexico. On the west end, she planted cactus and sandstone to resemble the llano. On the north and east, she rooted ponderosa pines from the forests. Along the southern edge, the Russian olive, salt cedar, river willow, and tamarisk of the Rio Grande bosque. One spring she decided to plant fruit trees to resemble the orchards of Corrales where she had strolled as a girl, hands sticky with nectar, surrounded by butterflies and bees. She took us kids to the nursery to pick our own saplings. My brother chose Bing cherries, dark, full of juice. My older sister selected baking cherries, bright red and sour. My middle sister and baby sister decided on peaches, giggling at the notion of fuzz. I chose apples, crisp as autumn air. In the center of our backyard I knelt beside my mother to dig the hole, rubbing dirt between my fingers like she did and patting down the root ball. I watered my sapling regularly and stared out my window waiting for the fruit, red and shiny, like a Christmas ball. Be patient, my mother said. Let it grow.

I wade through the weeds of my mother's backyard. Sweat stings my eyes in the mid-morning heat but I push forward anyway, determined to clear a path. After our trip to Seboyeta, I want to do something for her, say thank you in some way, so I've decided to clear the silver leaf maple overtaking her yard. Appraising the full height of the main trunk, which towers hydra-like from the southwest corner of her home, I wonder why she planted it in the first place. With ashen leaves and pale bark, it's so different than any of her other plants, colder than the earthy cottonwoods and rust-red Russian olives. I wonder if it reminded her of the aspens near Colorado bearing the markings of lonely shepherds. Maybe she planted it after my father died as a marker of that silent time. Or maybe she liked it precisely because it was different, because it stood apart. Whatever the reason, it's the most overgrown plant in an overgrown yard, with its tendrils choking away smaller shrubs.

I attack with a shovel, digging the roots, but the blade slides free from the slippery bark and bruises my ankle. I work harder, putting my back into it, as stubborn as these weeds about relinquishing the yard. From time to time, I feel my mother watching me through the back window, still wondering if I've found what I seek. I'm getting closer, I want to tell her. I can feel it.

After awhile she slips on cowhide gloves and joins me. We work side by side chopping and hacking and dodging the claw-like branches of a dead cherry tree looming above. When a branch scratches my cheek, I grumble about cutting it down. Squinting up at the dry bark, she nods.

On my way to the porch to retrieve a saw, I think about how the cherry tree was once the heartiest of five saplings we brought home from the nursery when I was little. Back in the yard, I steady the saw against the cherry branch and glance a few feet away at my tree, which looks just as dry and dead as the others, except for a few thin leaves on top.

"What happened to them?" I ask.

My mother sighs. Newcomers don't use the irrigation ditches anymore, she says, pulling crabgrass. Farmland became subdivisions. Irrigation dropped from once a week to once a month. She watered the fruit trees with the garden hose as long as she could, but during a drought after she had open-heart surgery, they became infested with carpenter ants and died.

I saw into the dusty bark. "Should I cut them all?"

"No." She points toward a leafless Russian olive tree sagging backward near a coyote fence. "Leave that one. My grandchildren like to climb it. It's not dead, yet."

Appraising the barren tree, I notice a rope looped around one of the branches as a swing.

"They love my yard just the way it is," my mother adds. "Wild."

She slips off her gloves and runs her fingers through the grass and extracts a walnut-sized chunk of white quartz, which she holds to the sun, wrinkling her nose. Standing on tiptoes, she places the stone between two Russian olive branches, smiling when she notices me watching.

"I like to leave treasures in my yard for my grandchildren. I call them, 'little jewels.' And you know what? They always know just where to find them."

She smiles at me and buries her fingers in the grass.

Midday. The sun beats down. While my mother rests inside I gather chopped roots and dead branches into a pile and turn my attention to the clusters of catnip filling the air with feathery pollen. I grip the stalks and pull by the root until my skin itches and my eyes water and I sneeze for several minutes straight. I push ahead anyway so I can finish before dark.

In a tangle of vines at the western edge of the yard I discover a long, low wooden bench with brown flaking paint—the antique my mother bought at auction in the early '70s before the city demolished the Alvarado Hotel, a century-old palace of red-tiled roofs, stone archways, brick footpaths, water fountains, and rose gardens. The Alvarado had been the gateway to the city, the crown jewel of the landmarks downtown. My mother visited the Alvarado often as a girl while her parents retrieved aunts and uncles arriving by train from Southern California. While the others waited in the depot, she settled back on one of these benches to watch travelers hurry toward one destination or another, perfectly content to sit on the sidelines as they passed, absolutely certain of who she was and where she belonged. After the auction, she sanded down the bench, repainted it, and set it on the front porch where she relaxed after supper while us kids played outside. When night fell and the streetlight flicked on at the curb, we could see her through the shadows, watching.

I pull the bench from the weeds and set it in the open.

Raking the catnip into piles, I discover more hidden artifacts—a stainless steel cooking spoon, a pair of tin snips, and a rose-colored teacup. I hold them in my hands. They're warm.

My mother used a long-stemmed spoon like this to stir our Christmas posole, the traditional hominy stew she simmered all day, filling the house with the aroma of pork, garlic, onions, olive oil, and oregano. Staring into the silvery surface, I imagine my younger self sneaking into the kitchen for a sip of the salty broth, windows fogged, holiday lights flickering amber, red, yellow, and blue.

I place it on the bench.

Tin snips. As a boy I watched my mother as she prepared for art shows, cutting sheets of copper and brass into bracelets and arm-bands etched with her "secret writings." She never told me what the symbols meant, or if she herself even knew, it was a language she spoke with her hands.

The rose-colored teacup feels as light as butterfly wings, with flower buds curling along its edges. I hold it to the sun and check for cracks. The surface is water-stained, but surprisingly intact. I recognize it from my mother's cupboard as one of her grandmother's Italian heirlooms. Looking through its pink tint, I picture the iron-haired woman sitting with my mother at a butcher-block table in the ranch house kitchen, savoring a sip of hibiscus tea while the llano wind hisses outside.

I place it on the bench with the others, gently as the offerings on a shrine.

By early afternoon the sky burns orange and red. My muscles ache, but I can see daylight through the weeds. Parting a particularly un-ruly chinaberry bush, I discover a small, faded blue plastic storage bin. I pop open the lid and stare into the face of my father.

Inside—snapshots, letters, holiday cards, and portraits, every-thing my mother packed into the hall closet decades ago. For several minutes I just stand there, baffled at how this long-lost box wound up outside. Maybe my mother moved it onto the porch, then the yard, and forgot. Maybe she knew exactly where it was, but figured since it was made of plastic, the contents were safe. Maybe she just wanted it out of the house all together. However it happened, the discovery seems almost too perfect, as if she wanted me to find it, like one of the "jewels" for her grandchildren.

Wiping my hands, I leaf through images I have never seen, im-ages I have always wanted to see—the two of them together, sitting on a couch, dressed for a party, hands touching, smiling sheepishly as though they've been caught kissing. Or this—a full-framed shot of our living room at Christmastime, the tree bedecked with bulbs and shimmering silver tinsel, bright with promise.

From the top of the stack, I lift a portrait of my father as a young man in a black business suit, white shirt, and black tie, his black hair slicked back and his Perry Mason eyes fixed forward. In all the photos

I have seen of him—all half-dozen of them—his expression has always been awkward, or his features blurred. But this image has been carefully composed. His shoulders are squared. His chin is held high. His cheeks are hand-tinted to a rosy glow. Here, he is smiling.

~

Dusk at last. A breeze of honeysuckle. After ten straight hours, I have managed to clear three-quarters of my mother's yard. As the weeds fell more relics appeared—a water bucket, a harvest sickle, a school bell—as though her yard were opening to me, revealing gifts. When I dig out the final maple root, she walks out to check on me, but pauses before a small wooden barrel exposed in the overgrowth. Parting the few remaining weeds, she peers inside, and places a hand on her chest.

"My fairy roses. I don't believe it. I thought they were gone."

She looks me in the eye. "Thank you for giving me my yard back."

I give her a quick squeeze. Setting aside the shovel, I begin to ask her about the bench, the rose-colored teacup, and the box of my father's things, but when she leans toward her flowers and holds one to her nose, I decide to leave it unexplained, another mystery of the house of seasons.

Peeling off my work gloves, I glance up at the apple tree. In a cluster of leaves near the top, a single fruit, bright red, ripe.

Charlotte's Web

HALF ASLEEP in my mother's spare room, resting after clearing her yard, I hear a voice outside on the front porch, "Get the Spanish sword. From the living room wall. Hurry."

My twenty-five-year-old niece clomps into the living room, screen door slamming behind her, then clomps back onto the porch, screen door slamming again.

"Good," my mother says. "Now stand back!"

Clang.

"Dang it, I missed. I can't see in this light."

"Let me try," my niece says. "You're too old for this."

Clang!

I find them on the porch on hands and knees, poking the sword behind a gutter spout.

"What are you doing?"

My niece screams. My mother drops the blade.

Blinking up at me, her eyes magnified through her bifocals, my mother explains: Black widow spiders have been creeping from her flower bed and into her den all summer, covering her artifacts in webs. In fact, while I was resting, she trapped one behind the spout.

"Just look at her," she says, shuddering. " Full of eggs. We have to get her."

"It's not doing anything."

My mother grips my arm. When she was a girl on the ranch, she says, one of her cousins woke up with a raging fever. The adults couldn't find anything wrong. Just as they were about to fetch the doctor, they rolled the seven-year-old onto her side and discovered, tucked in her armpit, a black ball with spindly legs and the telltale mark of a red hourglass.

"She nearly died," my mother whispers.

"Nearly died," my niece echoes.

They watch my face, waiting.

Rolling my eyes, I snatch up the sword, kneel on all fours, and come face to face with a spider as plump and shiny as a Spanish olive.

My niece screams.

I attack, jabbing and poking and parrying and thrusting before sliding the flat end of the ceremonial blade along the edge of the porch until I see a yellow stripe of spider juice.

My mother places a hand on her chest. "Thank you. Now I can rest."

I set the sword aside, heart pounding faster than I want it to, and stand.

"Watch out for Charlotte!"

My mother nudges me aside.

"Charlotte? Where?"

My niece twists a strand of blonde hair around her thumb.

"Go ahead. Show him."

My mother looks up at me and smiles.

"Promise you won't laugh."

After I promise, she points toward the cow skull wired to the porch viga. I squint into the blue evening light at a white dot suspended a few inches from my nose like a pearl on a chain.

The dot moves. Legs unfold. A crab. A skeleton. An alien.

I raise the sword.

"Charlotte!" my niece screams.

Snatching the blade from my hands, my mother tells another story: Charlotte is an orb spider who migrated from the irrigation ditch to her garden last spring and strung a web the size of a throw rug outside the dining room window. Each morning as the sun breaks over Sandia Crest, my mother pulls back her curtains to an octagon of silver and light.

"Most amazing thing you've ever seen."

She traces the design with her finger as if critiquing an Escher painting.

"See the geometrical pattern? The symmetry? Each day, Charlotte spins a new web for me. Hour after hour. She's so patient. And she eats all the bad bugs, too. Aphids. Gnats. Mosquitos. Unlike those horrible black widows, she's not harmful."

I step back and watch my mother's face, bright as the moon.

"Beautiful," she says. "Don't you think?"

"Yes," I tell her. "She is."

One Small Thing

THE SUN hangs over Corrales. Wood smoke drifts through the air. I kneel with my mother before Ernestina's grave at the village camposanto. She sets aside her pruning shears and slips on leather gloves while I open a garbage bag. With careful snips she trims the prickly pear that has completely covered her sister's small earthen plot with dozens of green pancake lobes and long white needles.

"I was afraid it would be like this," she says, tossing the trimmings into the bag. "After my surgery, I couldn't clean it out. I should have tried anyway."

I reach for a dried leaf near the headstone and jab my finger on a needle.

"Careful," my mother says. "Just hold the bag open. I'll do the rest."

Earlier that morning, I visited the graves of my grandparents, Desolina and Carlos, who are buried side by side several miles from the Sandia foothills. I brought American Beauties for her and a river stone for him. I also visited the plot of my great-grandmother, Adelida, and set white roses on her modest headstone near downtown Albuquerque. I stood before the grave of my mother's aunt, Molly, as well. I finally found her plot after sifting again through cemetery records. Her sunken plot, some fifty yards south from Adelida's, had been unmarked since she died in the train accident sixty years earlier. On it, I laid a bouquet of pink and white rosebuds, her favorite.

The flowers came from my mother's garden. She cut them herself and arranged them in vases filled to the brim with water so they might live awhile longer. I asked her to join me, but she shook her head, and I decided not to push it. If I could do this one, small thing for her, I would.

I said a prayer for each relative and thanked them for allowing me into their lives and into their stories. And I promised, as my mother has, to remember them.

As she works beside me now in the camposanto, she hums to herself, trimming the cactus she transplanted decades earlier from a roadside near Marquez. She chose prickly pear instead of irises, which Carlos favored, because she thought the cactus would thrive in direct sun, which it has.

I hear the sound again over my shoulder, the rustling of a lizard or a mouse I had heard on our earlier visit, and glance back toward the cemetery entrance where Serafina and Pablito are buried, somewhere in the weeds. I searched again for their lost graves, too, but decided, as my mother has, that it's probably best for her aunt and uncle to remain undisturbed, at least for a time.

After filling the bag with cactus clippings, my mother reaches beneath the white concrete headstone Carlos had made himself, and straightens the blue votive candle beneath the black hand-painted letters, "Ernestina," before pausing to caress a budding cactus blossom.

"In two weeks, this will be beautiful," she says. "My sister will be covered in red flowers."

Trying to smile, my mother reaches for a plastic gallon water jug she brought from home.

"Help me."

Together, we steady the jug, and pour.

I kill the headlights and roll onto the shoulder of the grassy field across from the adobe house in Corrales where my mother was born. Idling in park, I angle the wheel toward the road for a quick getaway. The sun has set. Crickets chirp in the weeds. Stepping into the dusky light, I slip under the barbed wire fence and approach the tree we saw earlier. My mother was right. It does hold fruit—a dozen small apples of yellow and red. I glance toward the road, then at the trailer with the sheet across the window. Holding my breath, I snatch the biggest apple I can find, and run to the car.

A half-hour later, I lean in the threshold of my mother's kitchen. She holds the fruit to the white glow of the ceiling bulb. She squints, sniffs, squints again, and scowls.

"What do you think?" I ask.

"Hush. Wait a minute."

Rubbing the apple on her apron, she takes a quick bite, chews. Her mouth forms a perfect "O."

Placing a hand on my shoulder, she closes her eyes.

"Manzanitas de San Juan."

My Honda creaks across the wooden bridge over the Rio Puerco, the shallow brown river cutting sixty feet deep through the rock and stone of the badlands. I stop dead center, glance over the edge.

"Jesus Mary and Joseph." My mother grips the dashboard with both hands. "What are you doing? You can't stop here. These bridges are old. Dangerous."

Staring into a gorge marbled with red and green sand, I try to explain: Before returning to Denver, I want to visit one last place from her stories—the river she always feared to cross.

"Yes," she says, facing me, eyes wide. "It was terrible. Now that you've seen it, let's go."

I steer across the rickety bridge and park on the shoulder.

My mother rolls up her window. "Don't stop here! There are sinkholes all around."

Looking left and right, unconvinced of the danger but not wanting to frighten her more, I pull forward another thirty yards and step out into the mid-morning heat.

"I want to see it for myself," I tell her. "I have to."

She locks her door. "Hurry!"

I break into a run. The Rio Puerco is the one place in my mother's stories, more than Corrales or even Marquez, that burns brightest inside me. It has always been the mythical gateway from the badlands to the valley, from the journey to the homecoming, from the land of the dead to the province of the living. I want to feel this ground for myself—to make it real, to make it my own.

Treading sand as thick as water, I pass the sinkholes my mother warned me about—dozens of bottomless black ovals spiraling like termite burrows through driftwood. One wrong step and I could twist an ankle, or worse. Staring down into a portal as deep as Alice's rabbit hole, I become dizzy, as if I'm sinking, my legs made of lead, passing from one dimension to another.

Before me on a white dune at the rivers' edge, I see a scattering of artifacts—broken glass, rusty nails, a half-buried gate, a palm-sized circle of barbed wire—placed like offerings on a shrine. For several minutes I just stand there, rooted in place, and in a shimmer of reflected light, I see him, Carlos, all dust and denim, standing between fence posts, gazing over the red gorge toward the green valley beyond, toward the only home he knows, toward his destination, his resting place.

A breeze stirs around me—an embrace—and everything starts to make sense. Maybe Carlos, cast adrift in his youth, found a sense of permanence in the yellow stone cliffs of Marquez. Maybe my mother, recovering from a lifetime of losses, found strength in the cycles of the llano. Maybe my family, called so strongly to the past, ventures into the desert not to chase memories, but to emerge from them, to awaken, to remind ourselves we are part of something larger, something deeper, something made of story as well as stone, something that will endure long after we have gone.

Home is a feeling. A faith. A way of seeing. A choice to belong. The land reminds us of that. It invites us to see what is—not what was—or what we want it to be. Maybe that's what Carlos tried to tell my mother in her kitchen all those years ago. The road back lies within. Each artifact is a compass of the heart. The loving wind is a warm current connecting us all to that place, no matter how far away we might travel. To find that vision, that presentimiento, I need only close my eyes.

My mother's voice rises above the ravine. I pick up the barbed wire and return to the car.

Removing her sunglasses, she studies me. "What did you see?"

I open my hand to reveal the gate loop.

She beams. "You found one. A key."

I scoop up the soil from my mother's yard and pack it into a two-gallon plastic bucket she places at my feet. I ask for a cutting of Roses de Castilla, but she decides instead to give me a shoot from the white lilac from Galisteo—the misplaced bush that somehow survived.

"Okay," she says. "Not too tight. Or else she won't be able to breathe. Like this. . ."

With strong bony hands she presses down the moist brown earth.

"Now watch. . ."

With the curved blade of her irrigation shovel, she draws a perfect circle around one of the shoots, leans into it with her full weight, pulls the handle, and digs up the root ball.

"Let me do that," I say, touching her shoulder. "You'll hurt yourself."

She waves me off.

"No. Get more dirt. Pack it around."

I get more dirt. Pack it around.

She lowers the shoot into the bucket. It looks like a palm tree on a desert island.

"Good," she tells me. "Now sprinkle more dirt around the roots. The soil from my garden will stop the poor little thing from going into shock when you plant her in Denver."

I sprinkle in more dirt.

"Good. Now help me," she says.

Together we raise a plastic water jug and pour an entire gallon onto the cutting.

"That should do it." My mother sighs. "She should be fine for your ride home."

I carry the transplant to my Honda and place it beside the yellow bloodstone from Marquez, the chamisal root from the Rio Grande, and the rusty barbed wire loop from the Rio Puerco. My mother leans over and tosses in her horseshoe, as well. A strand of gray hair falls across her face.

"Don't forget to water your lilac as soon as you get back," she says. "Give her a nice good soaking. Water her once a day for a week, then every few days after that, and use all the soil from my yard. That will help her sink new roots. In a season or two, she'll give you big, beautiful flowers."

She pauses, takes my hand, and looks up at me with her owl eyes.

"People, places, they are never lost to us. We will see them again, if only in our mind's eye."

Smiling, she fumbles in her housedress for a Mexican leather coin purse, slips out a white plastic vial of holy water, dips her thumb inside, and draws a cross on my forehead.

"Travel safely."

Epilogue

ONE AUTUMN afternoon at the landfill above Corrales, not far from her grandparents' old ranch, my mother stopped in the middle of raking dead leaves from the back of the pickup and glanced down at a pile of shriveled iris bulbs dumped on the roadside. "I can save them," she told my uncle. "I know I can." Once home, she dug a shallow trench in her backyard in the half-shade of the fruit trees and placed inside the fresh dirt a neat row of wrinkled brown tubers. The following spring, she woke to an explosion of pink, yellow, purple, and white. Gathering a bouquet, she stopped short at the sight of one blossom towering above the rest—an iris of the purist black. She thought she had transplanted a poisonous weed and fetched a shovel to dig it out. But as she approached the garden she set aside the blade. Above the new flower, a corona of butterflies and bees. On the breeze, the scent of orange, lemon, grapefruit, sunlight.

source notes

THIS IS a work of literary nonfiction. The characters, places, and events in this book are inspired by family stories and based upon memory, perception, and personal experience. Some names and identifying information have been changed or omitted to respect the privacy of others.

THE DEFINITION excerpts were compiled from numerous sources including Oxford Dictionaries, Urban Dictionary, Dictionary.com, and The Free Dictionary.

Excerpts on "Homing" were assembled from sources including a 1982 interview BBC "Naturewatch" with Robin Baker, *Animal Behavior* by Gretel H. Schueller and Sheila K. Schueller (Chelsea House Pub Library 2009), *The Homing Instinct: The Meaning and Mystery of Migration* by Bernd Heinrich (Houghton Mifflin Harcourt 2014), as well as the Oxford Dictionaries and Dictionary.com.

Excerpts on "Nostalgia" were assembled from "Nostalgia And Its Discontents," by Svenlana Boya, "When Nostalgia Was A Disease," by Julie Beck, *The Atlantic*, August 14, 2013, as well as the Oxford Dictionaries and Dictionary.com.

Information on Corrales was compiled from many sources, including the Corrales Historical Society, Village of Corrales Historical Preservation Committee, "A History of Corrales," by Lawrence Hill, and *Place Names of New Mexico* by Robert Julyan (University of New Mexico Press 1998).

Information on Seboyeta and Marquez were gathered through various sources including *The Place Names of New Mexico*, by Robert Julyan (University of New Mexico Press 1998).

Information on San Ysidro (St. Isadore) was compiled from various sources including The Catholic Encyclopedia, AmericanCatholic.org, Catholic Online, and *New Advent* Catholic Encyclopedia.

HARRISON CANDELARIA FLETCHER is an assistant professor in the MFA in Writing Program at Virginia Commonwealth University. His first book, *Descanso For My Father: Fragments of a Life*, won the Colorado Book Award for Creative Nonfiction and International Book Award for Best New Nonfiction, and has been taught in classrooms throughout the country.

His essays have appeared in many journals and anthologies including *New Letters*, *Fourth Genre*, *The Touchstone Anthology of Contemporary Creative Nonfiction,* and *Brief Encounters*, forthcoming from Norton in November 2015.

His honors include a *New Letters* Literary Award, a *Sonora Review* Nonfiction Award, a *High Desert Journal* Obsidian Prize, a Pushcart Prize Special Mention, and fellowships from the Arizona Poetry Center and Vermont Studio Center.

A native New Mexican, he lives with his wife and two children in Richmond, Virginia.

The Autumn House Nonfiction Series

Michael Simms, General Editor

Amazing Yoga: A Practical Guide to Strength, Wellness, and Spirit, Sean and
   Karen Conley

The Archipelago: A Balkan Passage, Robert Isenberg

Between Song and Story: Essays for the Twenty-First Century, Sheryl St.
   Germain and Margaret L. Whitford, eds.

Love for Sale and Other Essays, Clifford Thompson, 2012*

Bear Season, Katherine Ayres

A Greater Monster, Adam Patric Miller, 2013*

So Many Africas: Six Years in a Zambian Village, Jill Kandel, 2014*

Twin of Blackness: a memoir, Clifford Thompson

Presentimiento: A Life in Dreams, Harrison Candelaria Fletcher, 2015*

   *Winners of the Autumn House Nonfiction Prize

Design and Production

Cover and text design by Chiquita Babb

Cover art: "Presentimiento" by Harrison Candelaria Fletcher

Author photograph: Rebecca Allen

The text is set in Perpetua, a font originally designed by Eric Gill and cut by Charles Malin in 1928, for Monotype. Due to a series of difficulties, the font was not released to the public until 1932.

Printed by McNaughton & Gunn on 55# Glatfelter Natural